You've Been Holding It Together

Creating a Life You Don't Need to Escape From

Cherise Small, LCSW

Published by The Healing Point Therapy and Wellness

Los Angeles, California

ISBN: 979-8-234-09871-9

First Edition 2026

Printed in the United States of America

For permissions or inquiries:

Cherise@release2heal.com

Dedication

For Chris:

I want you to know that your worth will never require performance. Love will never demand concealment and holding everything together is not the price of mattering. Understand that feeling deeply is not weakness but that it is being human. Honor yourself with rest and never think asking for what you need is too much. Always understand that simply being you is enough.

For the women who raised me:

So much was carried without witness. Generations were held together through hands, silence, and endurance. This book belongs to the moments that went unrecognized. To the sacrifices made without applause and feelings buried to survive. What was given was everything that could be given. Your strength was taught long before it was named. And this work carries what you could not put down.

For the one still holding everything together:

The one who appears fine while slowly unraveling. The one who has been steady for so long that release feels unfamiliar. Exhaustion does not require explanation. Softness does not need to be earned. Falling apart does not erase worth. Neither does beginning again. What you carried was real, and what you survived mattered. Your presence remains.

Contents

A Note Before We Begin

Before you go any further, I want to say something directly to you.

This book is not a program. There is nothing to complete, no timeline to follow, and no version of yourself you are supposed to arrive at by the last page. What you will find in these chapters is an invitation to stop long enough to hear what you have been talking yourself out of for longer than you want to admit.

Some chapters will feel like they were written for you specifically. Others may not land until months from now, after a conversation you have not had yet or a moment that finally cracks something open. Come back to those. This book will be here.

At the end of each chapter you will find a section called Your Turn. These are not assignments. They are not a test. You do not have to answer every question, and you do not have to go in order. They are invitations to pause with what you just read and let it become personal. Some questions may feel too close. Others may feel irrelevant right now. Trust yourself to know which ones are asking something of you. Start there.

If writing feels hard, speak instead. Record a voice memo the way I did, in parking lots and bathroom stalls and at the edge of the bed after everyone else fell asleep. Say the things you have not been able to say out loud to another person. You might be surprised what comes through when you stop editing yourself before you even begin.

A few things worth knowing before you start:

This book is not therapy. The pages ahead will ask you to look honestly at patterns, name things you have been avoiding, and stay with discomfort you are used to moving through quickly. Some of what comes up may need more support than a book can hold. If you are experiencing severe depression, trauma, or thoughts of self-harm, please reach out to a licensed mental health professional. Asking for that support is not a detour from this work. It is part of it.

You do not have to read this alone. Some of the most honest conversations I have seen began with two people reading the same chapter and talking about it afterward. A trusted friend, a therapist, a partner, someone who has earned the right to hear you think out loud. This work does not have to happen in isolation.

You are allowed to feel whatever comes up while reading. Relieved. Resistant. Sad. Angry. Seen. Skeptical. None of it means you are doing it wrong. Every bit of it is information.

You are here. You opened this book and kept reading. You are not willing to keep going the way things have been. That is not a small thing, and it is not nothing. It is where everything begins.

Take your time.

-Cherise

Prologue

I was in my mother's apartment the first time I recorded a voice memo. I had come back home. It was not the way I had planned with a scheduled visit and a return flight booked. The way you returned when everything you had built fell apart and starting over was the only choice left. My son was asleep beside me, and I was crying quietly, pressing my face into the pillow so he would not wake up. I was already in therapy at that time. However, I needed something more honest than what I could say out loud to another person. Something I could only say to myself. So, I started recording voice memos on my phone. I called them, FEEL 2 BE FREE, because I knew in order to get through what I was experiencing, I couldn't run from it. I had to allow myself to sit in all the uncomfortable feelings.

This book began as voice memos. The ones I recorded at red lights when my hands were shaking. The ones I whispered in bathrooms while the world waited for me to pull myself together. I did not plan to share those moments. They documented the path from breakdown to breakthrough, from moving through the motions to being present, and from survival to something that finally felt like living a meaningful life.

But silence had a weight, too.

I recorded them because I had no one to tell. Because the weight I was carrying had no name yet. Because I thought if I could just say it out loud, even to myself, I might survive it.

I did survive it. Holding it together more was not the answer. Neither was becoming stronger, more disciplined, or more resilient. What saved me was admitting I was breaking. By naming the exhaustion no one else could see. The therapist who could not admit she needed therapy. The mother performing strength for a child who was already keeping score. Learning to identify what was mine to carry and what I had been holding for everyone else.

Somewhere in that disentanglement, I realized I was not alone. There are so many of us moving through the world this way, silently coming apart while showing up, functioning, pouring into others, and putting on a bright smile every single morning. All of us waiting for someone to say, "You do not have to keep holding it all."

This book is that permission.

Not permission to abandon your responsibilities, but permission to stop pretending and start naming what you are really holding. Permission to put down what was never yours, to understand rest without earning it, and to be honest even when honesty costs you the version of yourself others depend on.

I know what it costs because I paid it. Those voice memos I recorded between 2017 and 2024 were never therapy or journaling. They were a woman talking to herself in the dark because speaking the words aloud was the only way to make the weight real enough to name. The recordings lasted anywhere from thirty seconds to an hour. I would sit in parking lots, in bathroom stalls, on the edge of my bed after my son fell asleep, and I would just talk to no one in particular. Just because the alternative was keeping it all inside and I had been doing that long enough.

The first time I played one back I almost deleted it. What came through the speaker did not sound like the version of me I had been presenting to everyone else. It sounded like someone tired in a way that sleep could not touch — someone who had been carrying everything so long she had forgotten what putting it down felt like. I listened to the whole thing anyway. Sat with every word. Let it settle.

That was the beginning. There was no single revelation, only a woman finally willing to hear herself. And that is the invitation being extended to you here.

This is for the moments you smile while fading. The nights you cry without a sound and mornings you show up when your heart has not caught up yet. For everyone who has been told they were strong when what they needed was to be seen.

This book will show you what to do with that information. Not through checklists or wellness routines, but through the slow, uncomfortable work of learning to listen to yourself. To identify what is yours. All while letting go of what is not yours and building a life that does not require you to disappear to function.

The work begins with naming what you have been pretending not to see.

Some of what lives in these pages will ask more of you than a book can give. If that is where you are, get the support. Seeking help is not weak. It is the honest thing to do. Those recordings were the beginning of this book. But the story starts much earlier than that.

Introduction

Philadelphia gave me my foundation. Summers on the block with cousins running everywhere, water ice melting in paper cups. Water ice is a Philadelphia original, shaved ice packed sweet and cold, the thing you eat on hot steps because nowhere else does it the same way. Crab legs spread out on newspaper, everybody loud and laughing. We would race to Mr. Jimmy's window, the man on the block who sold penny candy and quarter treats out of his house, a neighborhood tradition that only exists where everybody knows everybody. Those were good days. Full days.

The women made all of it happen. They grilled, cooked, threw parties, and showed up for funerals and baby showers without being asked. They held the neighborhood together the same way they held their family together with their hands and their time and whatever they had left. The love was enormous and the laughter was pure.

But even at the grill, even in the middle of all that joy, there was always motion underneath it. Always someone ready to jump up and get something, handle something, check on someone. The stillness never came. Not really. They stopped when the body made them. But I never saw them slow down and just be. Rest was not part of the flow for the women in my family, but motion was.

As a child I was the quiet one on the steps watching all of it. Taking it all in the way children do, noticing things nobody named out loud. Words for what I was seeing did not exist yet. Something was always moving below the joy, and I felt it even when no one could say what it was.

That is where this book began, not in a therapy office. On those steps. Watching the people I loved most move through joy without ever landing in it.

Cherise Small LCSW was already forming.

The path toward therapy was not a choice. It was a calling.

What I saw on those steps never left me. Decades later I would sit across from someone in a therapy chair and feel it immediately, what the smile was covering, the exhaustion no one talked about. I knew what I was looking at because I had been watching it my whole life.

I am Cherise Small. Licensed Clinical Social Worker. Founder of The Healing Point Therapy and Wellness. I have spent a decade in a therapy chair listening to people describe a life that looks fine from the outside, but they feel like disappearing from the inside. I know that feeling. It is why I do this work.

I have sat across people who are dependable, capable, and exhausted in ways they cannot explain. Professionals who make complex decisions at work but cannot figure out why they cry in their cars. Parents who show up for everyone else but cannot remember the last time someone showed up for them. People who have built impressive lives that they are too exhausted to enjoy.

They come to therapy not because they have fallen apart, but because something inside them is whispering a question they are afraid to ask out loud, "Why does doing everything right still feel so wrong?"

Not just because I'm trained to see these patterns, but because I lived them.

I remember wiping down the same spot on the kitchen counter for the third time when I realized it — my hand was moving but I was not present. I could not remember what I had been thinking about. Could not remember the last time I had thought about anything that was not a task to complete or a need to meet. My apartment was small, the kitchen felt smaller. And I was disappearing inside of it.

I was three months postpartum, standing in an apartment in Maryland that was supposed to represent everything I had worked for. I had graduated with my master's degree, had gotten engaged, and relocated to a different state. Everything I had dreamed of was finally happening. I had the credentials. The relationship. The baby and the fresh start. But somewhere in the middle of achieving everything, I had stopped recognizing the person attaining it. I was becoming someone impressive and someone I did not recognize at the same time.

That kitchen counter moment was the moment I noticed something was off. There was no breakdown, no crisis. Just a normal Tuesday morning and the slow, creeping realization I had been moving through my own life for so long, I could not remember what it felt like to live it fully.

I did not have language for what was happening. I just knew something was off. I would wake up tired even after sleeping, forcing my smile through conversations while feeling completely disconnected. I would check off every item on my to-do list and still feel like I was failing. My son would look at me with those huge eyes needing me, but I was present in body and absent in every other way that mattered.

I told myself it was the adjustment period. I was a new mother living in a new state, starting a whole new life. But months passed and the heaviness did not lift. It settled deeper, became part of my baseline, and the background hum beneath everything I did.

I remember standing outside a Safeway in Baltimore one evening, grocery bags in hand, waiting to be picked up. I stood there on the phone with my best friend, talking but not present. I watched cars pull in and out of the parking lot. It took me several minutes to remember I had driven myself. The keys were in my bag the whole time. I had been so far outside of myself; I did not know where I was. I had everything I had worked for. I just could not feel any of it.

At the time, I did not have language for it, but I was experiencing what I now call the quiet crash. The breakdown that hides inside success and is mistaken for dedication by everyone watching.

Nobody checks on the one who always shows up.

What I know now, after years of doing the work both clinically and personally, is that the crash was not about that relationship, that apartment, or even new motherhood. It was about the pattern. The one where I had been holding it all together for so long, I could not remember what it felt like to let go. I turned motion into my entire personality and used exhaustion as proof I was trying hard enough.

The difference between me and my clients back then was that I had the training to name what was happening. I understood nervous system dysregulation. But naming it did not stop it.

Awareness alone does not rewire a nervous system that has been conditioned to associate rest with danger and motion with survival.

I could teach regulation all day and still go home dysregulated. I helped others set boundaries while abandoning my own. I could spot the signs that a client was unraveling within five minutes but miss them entirely in myself. That is the painful irony of being a therapist who needs therapy: you know exactly what you should be doing and still cannot make yourself do it. Knowing better and doing better are not the same thing.

So, I did something I had been avoiding. I stopped moving long enough to feel it.

I sat with the burning. The fear. The shame of admitting I was not fine when my entire professional identity was built on helping other people be fine. I went to therapy myself, which felt like failing even though I knew intellectually it was not. I studied my own nervous system the way I observed my clients, tracking my patterns with the same clinical detachment I used on a case study.

After that quiet crash, I moved to Los Angeles with my son to pursue my dreams. Not to run from what broke me, but to build something from it. I founded my private practice, The Healing Point Therapy and Wellness, helping people recognize the signs early, to teach them what I had to learn the hard way: you do not have to fall apart first.

But the work did not stop when I moved. It took years. Years of unlearning the belief my worth was measured by how much I could carry. Long nights teaching my body stillness was not dangerous. Early mornings rewriting the story that said rest was something I had to earn through breaking down. And most importantly, years of learning that healing is not linear, setbacks are not failures, and the nervous system remembers patterns long after the mind decides to change them.

And now, on the other side of that work, I live in what I call the BLISS Rhythm.

I did not design the BLISS Rhythm from a textbook or a training. It emerged from the years I spent learning what my body was trying to tell me before I knew how to listen. It came from the mornings I sat with discomfort instead of running from it, the boundaries I held when everything in me wanted to give in, and the slow realization that peace was not something that happened to me. It was something I had to practice on purpose.

The BLISS Rhythm is not perfection or a permanent state of calm where hard days do not exist. It is a rhythm I can trust. One that helps me create a life where I know what I need and when I need it. Where I can feel my body asking me to pause before it forces me to stop. It is where rest is not something I negotiate or earn through suffering. It is something I practice because I finally understand it is not optional.

Some days are easy. Some days the old pattern reaches for me, that familiar pull toward productivity and motion. But I do not disappear anymore or lose months going through the motions. I know what peace feels like now. Not the version I performed for everyone else. The real kind. And I know how to find my way back when I drift.

What you will find in these pages is what I learned sitting in therapy, sitting with clients, and sitting with myself when I could not run anymore. You will see how patterns take root, how they are mistaken for strength, and how to move through them without burning your life down. This is not theory. It is what worked when nothing else did.

The framework that guides this book is something I call the BLISS Rhythm: Breathe and Listen, Identify and Soothe, Sustain. It is not a checklist you complete once and move on. It is a rhythm you return to repeatedly whenever you notice you have stopped breathing, stopped listening, stopped feeling.

Breathe and Listen is about recognizing when your nervous system is activated and learning to pause instead of reacting. It is the foundation, the thing that makes everything else possible.

Identify and Soothe is about distinguishing what is yours to carry from what you have been holding for everyone else, then learning to regulate without abandoning your needs.

Sustain is about what happens when you fall back into old patterns...because you will. It is about returning, rebuilding, and trusting the work you have done does not disappear just because you had a hard week.

We will move through recognition, honesty, boundaries, pause, inheritance, setbacks, and rhythm. You will learn the difference between moving through the motions and feeling present, between enduring and evolving, and between surviving and living.

This work is not about becoming unbreakable. It is about becoming whole. You will learn to stay connected to yourself while navigating stress, not eliminate it, and how to finally inhabit your life instead of escaping it.

The chapters ahead will ask you to look at patterns you have normalized, question beliefs you have inherited, and practice skills that feel uncomfortable at first. This will not be easy. But it will be worth it.

I wrote this book as a clinician and as a person who has lived every chapter of it. The woman wiping down the kitchen counter for the third time; standing outside a Safeway not knowing she had driven herself there; three months postpartum in an apartment that was supposed to represent everything, feeling nothing. That was me. I am not writing from the other side of a clean transformation. I am writing from the other side of years of showing up for my own life even when it was hard, even when the old patterns came back, even when I had to start over. That is what I want for you. Not a perfect life, but a life that finally feels like yours.

You have been holding it together long enough. Let us find out what happens when you stop.

Part One
Recognition

"Freeing yourself was one thing; claiming ownership of that freed self was another."

-Toni Morrison

Chapter 1
The Smile That Hides the Weight

"I'm fine."

Everyone says it, and most days you believe it. You show up on time, meet the deadlines, answer the texts, and smile through the exhaustion. People depend on you. You are the one holding everything together when everyone else is allowed to fall apart. From the outside, you are exactly what everyone needs you to be. And that is the problem.

But inside, something is breaking.

You can feel it in the heaviness in your chest that never quite releases. In the way rest feels like guilt. The type of tiredness that sleep does not touch. You are tired in a way you cannot explain to people who think being tired means needing a nap. This tired lives deeper. It is in your bones, in your breath, you have forgotten what it feels like to be still without your mind racing toward the next thing you have not done yet.

Something has felt off for a while now, and if you are being honest, you have known it longer than you want to admit. But every time you get close to naming it, sitting with it long enough to understand what you need, something pulls you back into motion. Another email arrives, another person needs something, and the crisis that was supposed to be temporary has become the baseline. It is easier to keep moving than it is to stop and feel what is waiting in the stillness.

So, you keep going. You convince yourself you will rest later after this project, after this season, after you prove you can manage it all. But later never comes. And the tiredness starts to feel less like a phase and more like who you are.

The people who live like this rarely notice when the change happens. The body begins to whisper long before it screams. The way you carry yourself shift, there's less room to exhale, your laughter changes shape. What begins as stress becomes a busy season, and a busy season becomes your personality. Eventually it is simply who you are: high capacity, reliable, the one who can handle anything. Hiding fatigue behind presentation becomes fluent, automatic, and eventually you stop noticing you have not felt ease in months because tension has become your resting state. When the body learns movement keeps you safe, it keeps you moving, even when the danger has passed. You are functioning without being present. Managing without feeling. Moving through a life you have stopped inhabiting.

I see this pattern everywhere now. At the grocery store, watching someone organize their cart while on a work call. At the coffee shop, the person who cannot sit down until the laptop is open. Even my eight-year-old notices it. One day he asked, "Mom, why do grown-ups always look so busy even when they are not doing anything?"

When clients sit across from me and say, "I am just tired," I know they are not talking about sleep. I can see it in the way their shoulders curve forward, protective. The way they pause mid-sentence and lose their train of thought. How their hands stay busy, adjusting their sleeves, picking at the cuticles, reaching for water they do not drink. Their eyes look clear enough, but something behind them has dimmed. They are barely present. The exhaustion shows in the flatness of their voice, the way laughter does not reach their face, and they apologize for taking up space even though they are paying to be in that space.

This is not the kind of tiredness that rest touches. It is the weight of unexpressed emotion, the fatigue that comes from being the first in the family to want something different, or the only one in the office who cannot afford to fall apart. The fatigue of living in emotional autopilot. You wake up every morning determined to make it through the day, and before you know it, years have passed and you have built an entire identity around endurance. Some become anxious, overstimulated by the constant demand to stay on. Others go numb, moving through the world like they are watching it from behind glass. Either way, the body pays the cost.

The world rewards people who appear unbothered. It claps for the woman who does it all, the man who never cracks, and the professional who never drops the ball. But every "I have got it" costs something. You pay in fragments, moments of tenderness you do not have time to feel, meals eaten standing up, joy postponed until later. And later never comes because life keeps handing you new reasons to stay composed. Yet, intimacy thins when usefulness becomes identity.

If you enter a room scanning for tasks before you check your own pulse, you know this story. It is not about weakness or lack of gratitude. It is about training. Somewhere along the way, we learned being needed is safer than being known. We learned calm must be earned, love is confirmed through labor, and stillness is suspicious. Some of that training came from family systems that rewarded helpfulness and punished need. Workplaces celebrated the ones who never said no. Culture finished the job by teaching us to treat depletion as dedication and rest as indulgence. The result is a generation of people who look put together but are gradually unraveling under the weight of their own reliability.

For years, I thought the goal was to become unshakeable, to handle the pressure without letting anyone see the cracks. But you cannot out-organize what you refuse to feel. Headaches became my morning alarm. Anxiety became caffeine. Smiles became armor. I called it balance. It was survival dressed as discipline.

Here is what I have learned: strength built on suppression is not strength, it is tension. It breaks softly. The people around you may never see it happen because you are skilled at keeping your voice even, your posture upright, your schedule busy enough to outrun self-awareness. There is no explosion. You simply disappear inside your own competence until you cannot tell where the act ends and the person begins.

Sometimes the breaking does not look like falling apart. It looks like folding towels you do not need to fold at midnight because stillness feels dangerous. Or checking your phone again for messages you already read because silence makes your heart race. It looks like another degree, another project, another relationship that keeps you from hearing yourself think. The world praises this kind of productivity. It will call you ambitious, strong, dependable, but it will never ask what it is costing you.

I remember standing in front of the mirror one morning, fastening my watch, putting on earrings, assembling the armor I wore to look like I had it all under control. I looked fine.

More than fine, even thriving. And that is when it hit me: the most dangerous depletion is the one that hides inside success. It looks like achievement and sounds like gratitude. It convinces you that you are lucky to have so much to manage.

That morning, I was running late. Just enough that I had to decide whether to eat breakfast or answer the three emails that had come in overnight. I chose the emails. I stood at the kitchen counter scrolling while my coffee went cold for the second time that week. My son was getting ready in the next room. I heard him moving around, getting himself dressed. He had learned not to need me in the mornings. I had not noticed that until right then.

I walked back to the mirror to finish getting ready and stopped. Just stopped. Looked at the woman looking back at me. Credentials on the wall. A full calendar. Everything in order. And a tiredness so deep it had stopped feeling like tiredness and started feeling like personality.

That was when I understood it. A slow, heavy knowing sitting in my chest. The kind that has been true for a long time and has been waiting patiently for you to stop moving long enough to feel it. My hands slowed on the counter. My throat tightened. I stood there in the same bathroom where I had performed composure every single morning and felt the full weight of how long I had been doing it. Long enough that I could not remember when it started.

I finished getting ready. I drove to work. Held my sessions and answered my emails and said yes to things I should have said no to. The armor stayed on. But something underneath it had cracked open. And once you feel that kind of crack, you cannot go back. That morning was the beginning of me finally admitting I was tired. Not to anyone else. Just to myself, in the quiet of a bathroom that had watched me pretend for years.

One Sunday, Chris and I drove down to the beach for no reason. We did not have an agenda. Just wanted to see the ocean. We got ice cream, walked the boardwalk, and watched the skaters. On the drive back, with the windows down, he said, "Mom, we should do nothing more often." I looked at him in the rearview mirror. He was smiling and so was I. Turns out, doing nothing with someone you love is not nothing at all.

This is how so many of us live: functional, responsible, and gently detached from our own aliveness. We tell ourselves we are grateful. We say other people have it worse. And that is true. But comparison does not heal depletion. It just teaches you to ignore your own capacity. You cannot pour from an empty cup, but some of us learned to pour from a cracked one and call it generosity.

The problem is not that we care too much. It is that we care unevenly. We protect everyone else's peace while abandoning our own, make everyone else comfortable while suffocating under politeness, and somewhere in all of that we confuse control with safety and busyness with purpose.

Forgetting to exhale looks like this: a tightness across your chest that never quite releases, even when the day is over. Shoulders that never drop, even in sleep. Breath that sits high in your chest instead of reaching your belly. Coffee gone cold on your desk because you have not had a moment to drink it. You move from task to task without pausing, as if the space between doing might swallow you whole.

When I first began noticing the cracks, I did not know what to do with them. My body did not know how to be safe without productivity to prove my worth. It took time to learn I was conditioned. Conditioned to prioritize image over intuition, to solve instead of softening. Most of us are. It is not a personal flaw. It is a collective inheritance. We come from lineages where survival was the only option and pausing was a luxury no one could afford. The world has changed. Rest is repair now, not rebellion.

If this sounds familiar, you are not alone. The exhaustion you feel is not proof you are failing. This is evidence you have been operating without a margin for too long. Every system, body, business, and relationship requires recovery to function properly. We have been trained to see recovery as optional, indulgent, or selfish, but recovery is what sustains capacity and keeps compassion from hardening into resentment.

Many of us were not taught to rest. We were taught to recover just enough to resume the role. Real rest is different. It is not a reward for perfect days. It is part of how a life becomes livable. When recovery is built into the day rather than bolted on at the end, strength stops being an act and starts being a way of moving.

You are allowed to slow down without losing progress. You are allowed to feel without apologizing for it. You are allowed to want a life that does not require constant resilience to survive.

Stopping the performance may make you unrecognizable to yourself at first. The quiet will feel wrong, even frightening. You will be tempted to fill it with noise, to reach for the phone, to plan another task. But stay with it. The discomfort you feel is not emptiness. It is space. And that space is what restoration requires.

Here is what changed: I started noticing jacarandas. They bloom purple in May all over Los Angeles, and I had been driving past them for years without ever really seeing them. One afternoon I pulled over and just sat there looking at one, purple spilling everywhere, messy and beautiful in a way that felt almost deliberate. A woman walking her dog smiled at me like she understood. Maybe she did.

There is a moment, somewhere between exhaustion and awareness, where the truth finally lands. What carried you through was endurance mistaken for stability, survival mistaken for strength. That distinction matters. Survival was the bridge, not the destination. You crossed it because you had to. But you do not have to build your house there.

You have been operating at capacity for so long that moving on fumes started to feel like the baseline. The cost shows up in ways most people never see: the vacancy that crosses your face when someone asks how you are, the moment you stop expecting anything for yourself, the growing distance between who you are and who you have had to become to keep everything running.

You see it now. That is where the real change begins.

Your Turn

You have been performing for so long that the performance stopped feeling like a choice. These questions are not asking you to fix anything. They are asking you to look. Pick one and stay with it without reaching for an explanation. What is true does not need to be polished to be useful.

1. What are you most afraid will happen if you stop performing? Write the worst-case scenario. The thing you do not say out loud.

2. What does your body do when you are about to say yes to something you do not want to do? Write what your body knows before your mouth agrees.

3. Finish this sentence honestly: I have been pretending that I am fine, but the truth is...

4. If someone followed you around for a week and watched how you actually live, not how you describe your life, what would they see that you never talk about?

5. Finish this sentence: I keep saying I will rest when... but the truth is, I am scared that if I stop...

Chapter 2
The Mirror Does Not Lie

The night before I admitted I was tired, I stood in the bathroom, face-to-face with a woman I no longer knew. The light was too bright, and the silence was heavy. There was no collision, no breaking point, only the stillness that comes when your body has been whispering for years and you have run out of ways to pretend you cannot hear it. I looked at my reflection, not to fix my face, but to see if I was still in there. That is the strange thing about performing. It allows you to function so well; you don't notice when you have gone missing.

I used to think change would come with a plan, something I could measure or control: a new job, a new schedule, or new version of discipline. But real change rarely announces itself. It does not ask permission. It arrives gently, through depletion, one small moment when the cost of pretending becomes heavier than the fear of beginning again. It is not glamorous or linear. It is inconvenient, humbling, and sometimes quiet. That is why most people turn away from it because the first thing transformation asks for is honesty, and honesty is rarely comfortable.

There is a lie people tell about strength, that it looks like certainty. In truth, strength often begins with disorientation. It shows up as restlessness and discomfort long before it feels like clarity. For me, it began with a low hum beneath everything I did. I was meeting deadlines, keeping promises, showing up for everyone who needed me. Still, I would come home and feel a knot in my chest, like I was holding my breath in a life that no longer fit. When I told a friend I was fine, I meant it the way people meant it when they are afraid the truth will make things fall apart.

The mirror became my checkpoint. Every morning, I stood there, trying to smooth the exhaustion from my face and convincing myself I was strong. It took me years to understand I was not strong. I was rehearsed.

Being rehearsed costs something different than being strong. Strength, real strength, has a bottom to it. A place where you can rest and refill. Rehearsal has no bottom. It just has the next performance. The next morning you wake up and assemble yourself again. The same tone. The same posture. The same answer when someone asks how are you doing. You get so good at it the people closest to you stop asking follow-up questions. They take the performance at face value and move on. And some part of you is relieved because explaining the truth would take more energy than you have left.

The smile I gave the world was not real. It was practiced, perfected over time. The light tone I used when someone asked how I was doing. The way I could pivot a conversation away from my own struggle without anyone noticing. The posture I held shoulders back, chin up, even when my body wanted to give out. None of it was strength. It was performance so polished it looked like confidence.

I had rehearsed my way through grief, through disappointment, through depletion that should have stopped me. I knew exactly how to make '*I am fine*' sound convincing even when I was falling apart.

A client came in after landing a major promotion. When I congratulated her, she smiled and said, "Thank you, it is such an honor." Perfect delivery. But her shoulders were near her ears. Her hands were folded tight in her lap. I waited. She kept talking about the opportunity, the team, the responsibility. All the right words in all the right order. Finally, I interrupted her. "You just got the thing you have been working toward for three years. How do you actually feel about it?" She stopped mid-sentence. Stared at me. Then said, "I do not know. I have not checked." That is when I realized she was not avoiding the feeling. She did not know how to access it anymore. The performance had become so practiced it had replaced the person.

There is a difference between endurance and evolution. Endurance helps you survive what is breaking. Evolution asks you to stop performing the pattern altogether. That space between the two is where everything changes. It is the moment when you realize what landed you here cannot take you further.

One afternoon, a client sat across from me and said, "I am afraid that if I stop being the one who holds everything together, everything will fall apart." Her words landed on me like a mirror. I could see it in her. The depletion that looks like stability. The loyalty to dysfunction that keeps people from changing. We both knew what she meant. She was not afraid of the fall. She was afraid of who she would be without the weight. When you have been defined by what you carry, setting it down feels like losing yourself.

That is the part most people do not talk about. Growth sounds inspiring until you are the one doing it and change sounds beautiful until it asks you to release the very habits that once kept you safe.

For a while, I tried to negotiate with change instead of surrendering to it. I added a morning routine without changing what the morning was for. I started meal prepping on Sundays, like structure was the same thing as peace. I downloaded the meditation app, set the reminders, and felt guilty every time the notification appeared because I had not opened it in three days. I told myself I was building healthy habits. What I was doing was giving my need for control a wellness aesthetic. The schedule looked different. The weight was identical. I was wrong about what the problem was. You cannot reorganize your way out of something that requires honesty.

There came a night when I sat in my car outside my apartment and could not bring myself to get out. The world kept moving, but I was done pretending I could keep up. That was the moment I understood change does not begin when things get easy. It begins when you stop fighting the truth that it is not supposed to be easy. Ease comes after honesty, not before it.

I sat in that car for a long time. The engine was off. The parking lot lights were on, and everything outside looked the same as it always did. Normal. Ordinary. Nothing about that evening announced itself. There were no tears, no revelation, only the quiet certainty of someone who was just done. Done managing the gap between how I looked and how I felt. Done performing steadiness for people who had never once asked what it was costing me. I did not have a plan. I did not know what came next. I just knew I could not keep pretending the weight was not there. That was not a breakthrough. It was a release. The first real one in longer than I could remember. Sometimes that is all change needs to begin. Just one moment where you stop lying to yourself long enough to feel the full weight of what you have been carrying.

In that moment I realized change did not arrive in a grand breakthrough. It came through quiet decisions. Not answering a call that drained me, closing the laptop before midnight, saying I cannot this time and resisting the urge to explain why. Each one felt like rebellion at first. Over time, they started to feel like repair. That is the quiet transformation no one celebrates, the kind that does not look like success but feels like peace finally choosing what is best for you.

What nobody tells you about choosing differently is how uncomfortable it is at first. Those quiet decisions did not feel like growth. They felt like betrayal. Every time I said no, the guilt arrived immediately, loud and familiar. It told me I was selfish, difficult, and that I was going to lose people I loved. Some days I believed it. I would hold the boundary in the morning and spend the afternoon questioning it. But I kept going, not because I was certain, but because I was tired of the alternative. And slowly, something deeper began to stabilize. My body started noticing the difference between the exhaustion that comes from overextending and the discomfort that comes from growing. They feel different. One depletes and the other builds. Learning to tell them apart was the lesson.

One Saturday morning, I slept until 10 am without setting an alarm. When I woke up, my first thought was not guilt but shock. I had forgotten what it felt like to wake up rested instead of just less tired. Chris knocked on my door around 10:30. *"Mom, you okay?"* I laughed. *"Yeah, baby. I am just sleeping."* He paused. *"That is good. You never sleep this late."* He said it so matter-of-factly, like he had been keeping track. Maybe he had been.

Necessary does not mean easy. It means honesty. It means you stop disappearing into other people's comfort in the name of being likable or fine, stop mistaking depletion for dedication, and start living in a way that feels like yours, even when everyone who benefits from your exhaustion calls it selfish.

Change will always ask something of you. It will ask for comfort, certainty, and sometimes applause. What it gives back is ownership, the quiet kind that does not need validation to exist. Freedom does not come from doing more. It comes from doing what is true, even when it is misunderstood. None of it was easy or glamorous. It was necessary. And necessary was enough to begin.

Your Turn

The most dangerous thing about a practiced performance is how convincing it becomes, even to the person giving it. These questions are asking you to step outside of it for a moment and say something honest. You do not need to have it figured out before you begin. Being willing to look is enough.

1. What behavior have you been practicing for so long it feels automatic? When did you start performing it and why?

2. Write down the story you have been telling yourself about why you cannot change yet. Then read it back and ask: is this true or is this fear dressed up as logic?

3. Think about the version of yourself you show at work, with family, and with friends. Which one is closest to who you actually are when you are alone? Which one is the furthest?

4. When was the last time you stopped performing long enough to feel? What happened when you did?

5. What would you have to grieve if you admitted you were exhausted? What story about yourself would you have to let go of?

Chapter 3
Where Did I Go?

Hiding means you are still there. Disappearing means you stopped noticing when you left.

There are seasons when you move through your days and realize you no longer recognize the sound of your own voice. You wake up, handle the lists, answer the calls, and make the meals, and it all blurs into a rhythm of obligation. The noise of the world grows louder, but inside something has gone quiet. You have learned to function so well that no one can tell you have been missing from your own life, living in motion but detached from meaning, completing every task like muscle memory while wondering, in the still moments, when did I disappear?

It does not happen suddenly. It happens in small choices that seem harmless at first. The *"Sure, I can do it,"* when you want to rest. The smile that hides your exhaustion. The way you say you are fine because explaining feels like work. Each moment erodes a small piece of truth, and before long you have built a life that runs smoothly on the surface but feels hollow underneath. You tell yourself this is adulthood, responsibility, and strength. But strength without self-awareness becomes disconnection in disguise.

There was a time when I thought losing myself meant falling apart. I know better now. You do not always break when you are lost. Sometimes you perform with precision. You show up on time, you meet expectations, and you even collect praise. But what the world calls dependable, your body knows it as slow damage. The silence that follows an accomplishment is not peace. It is distance. The nervous system learns to mute what it cannot support. It calls it calm, but it is really absence, the body's way of conserving energy when the soul is tired of negotiating its needs.

The cost of disappearing shows up in ways you do not expect. It shows up in the flatness of your voice when your child asks about your day. In the way joy feels like work instead of relief. In relationships that exist on autopilot, where you are present but not actually there. You are efficient and capable, but somewhere along the way, you stopped feeling connected to the life you are managing. That is the real loss, not the breakdown. It's the slow fade into function without feeling.

I remember sitting in my car after a long day of sessions, the air conditioning humming against the static in my mind. I had spent hours helping others make sense of their emotions, yet mine felt like a language I had forgotten. The thought came quietly, *what would be left if I stopped moving?*

I sat there with my hand on the key, unable to turn the engine off. Not because I was tired, but because going inside meant facing the silence. The type of silence that asks questions you have been avoiding. Who are you when no one needs you? What do you want when there is no one to perform for? The questions felt too big, so I stayed in the car, scrolling through my phone, pretending I was doing something productive, but I was really delaying the moment of being alone.

One day, I was between sessions when my phone died. It went completely dead, mid-scroll in a coffee shop I had ducked into for a quick caffeine hit. The barista was making my latte like she had nowhere else to be. Measuring, steaming, pouring that design into the foam with deliberate slowness. There was nowhere to look, nothing to check, no next thing to mentally prepare for. So I looked at her hands. The precision and focus. When she slid the cup across the counter my whole body had gone still, not from stress but from presence. For thirty seconds I had been somewhere else. That question I had been avoiding in the car returned, *what would be left if I stopped moving*? Sitting in that coffee shop I got my first honest answer. Not much. And that was the beginning.

That moment stayed with me for weeks. I was not depressed or fine. I was somewhere in between, suspended in the gray space where accomplishment disguises exhaustion. A weird space where achievement becomes armor and stillness feels like failure.

I often see that same exhaustion in therapy sessions. Clients describe the weight of being the one everyone depends on. That heavy mix of pride and fatigue, the ache of being indispensable but invisible. I tell them what I had to learn myself: detachment is not peace. It is a body trying to survive its own overextension. When you have been on for too long, the mind confuses shutdown for rest.

The cure is not more productivity. It is permission. Permission to rest before you have earned it, to say no without justification, to feel something without immediately reaching for a fix.

It took me a while to understand that permission is a muscle, not a mindset. You strengthen it through practice: saying no without apology, sitting still even when your mind tells you to get up, taking a deep breath and letting it count as something. For many of us, that homecoming takes the longest. The difficulty is never knowing what to do. It is in believing our worth is not conditional on how much we give.

I started noticing small signals I was beginning to return. The first was awareness, the type that interrupts autopilot. I caught myself before agreeing to something I did not have the energy for. I paused before filling silence with productivity. And when guilt showed up, as it always does, I met it with curiosity instead of compliance.

In those moments something settled. Not everything at once. Just enough to remind me I was still here and that I could still choose.

A group text came through. Someone was organizing a committee, and my name was already volunteered before anyone asked me. That is how automatic it had become. Not just my yes, but other people's assumption of it. My fingers moved to reply before I had even decided how I felt. But something stopped me, not logic or strategy, just a soft voice that said you do not have to. The phone went down without explanation or apology. The guilt showed up immediately, hot and familiar, and this time I did not run from it. Instead of running from it, I sat with it. I asked myself, *what am I afraid of.* The answer was honest: that saying no makes me less valuable. That rest makes me selfish. That my worth depends on my availability. Those beliefs did not disappear but naming them loosened their grip.

I was walking to my car after a long session when I heard a saxophone. A street performer playing something slow, no case open, no ask, just sound moving through the air. My body stopped before my mind decided to. Not because I loved jazz or had time to spare, but because something in me needed to. For one full minute I stood there on the sidewalk and felt something I had not accessed in months, appreciation that was not attached to productivity. I was not analyzing it, planning to tell someone, or checking my watch. I was just there. When he finished, I walked away without taking a photo or making it into a story. Just a minute of my life where I existed without purpose, and somehow that was enough.

Being disconnected from yourself is not a flaw. It is a consequence of living in a world that rewards depletion. But once you see what silence has cost you, choosing differently becomes possible. Rebuilding from presence instead of pressure becomes possible. Returning to your own life piece by piece with tenderness and truth instead of performance becomes possible, too.

Maybe that is what healing really means. Not escaping your responsibilities or reinventing your identity but remembering your voice deserves to be heard even in the noise. Peace is not a reward for doing everything right. It is what becomes available when you stop making yourself the last priority in your own life.

When you reach that stillness, stay there. Do not rush to fill it. Let it teach you. Trust it enough to let it become your compass. Recognition is not the finish line. It is the first honest step. Seeing the pattern is significant but seeing it does not release you from it. What releases you is understanding where it came from, who taught it to you, and why you accepted it as your own. That requires a different kind of courage. The kind that finally lets you stop long enough to ask the questions you have been outrunning your entire life.

Your Turn

Losing yourself is rarely loud. It happens in small, quiet decisions over a long period of time, and most people do not notice until they have been gone for a while. These questions are not about blame. They are about finding where you are. Start wherever feels most true.

1. Sit with this question for five minutes without scrolling, without moving, without doing anything. Write whatever comes up, even if it is messy. When did I stop mattering to myself?

2. Think about a decision you made in the last month. Did you ask yourself what you wanted or did you just figure out what would cause the least disruption for everyone else? Be honest.

3. Write down three things you used to love before life got this heavy. Then write why you stopped doing them. Was it time or was it guilt?

4. If you could say one true thing to the person who relies on you most, what would it be? The thing you have been holding back because you are afraid it will hurt them or change everything.

5. Finish this statement: I stopped recognizing myself when I started believing that...

Part Two
Understanding

"The weight was never yours to begin with. You just never got the chance to put it down."

- Cherise Small, LCSW

Chapter 4

It Was Never About Being Good Enough

For years, I thought the exhaustion belonged to me. The voice in my head saying keep going just a little more, the reflex to say yes when I meant no, the guilt that rose every time I rested. All of it felt like mine. Like I was the one who decided worth had to be earned, rest had to be justified, and stillness was a luxury I had not worked hard enough to deserve.

One day, I was on the phone with my mother when I heard it in her voice. Not what she was saying, but the way she was saying it. That heaviness that comes from being tired in your bones. The kind of tiredness that lives underneath the words, making everything sound like it is being pushed uphill. She was telling me about her day, about what she handled, and about who needed what when something in me went still. Listening to her, I was not just hearing my mother. I was hearing myself ten years from now.

I knew that voice. I had been using it myself for months, maybe years. The tone that says I am fine while everything underneath quietly gives way. The steadiness performed for everyone else while running on fumes. I thought I had invented it. But here it was in my mother's voice, like she had taught me the script without either of us knowing.

That is when I realized: this weight was never mine to begin with.

I come from women who love hard, women who believe their worth is measured by how much they can carry. They show up without question, even when it costs them everything. Giving until there is nothing left, then figuring out how to give some more. These are women everyone adores: dependable, strong, the kind you can count on in any season. They are all those things. But what I noticed, even before I had language for it, was how little they kept for themselves.

I remember watching my grandmother move through the house at the end of a long shift, still finding things to do. Dishes that could wait, laundry that could sit, but she kept moving, like stopping meant failure. The parties, the laughter, the way she had let loose for a few hours, none of it touched the exhaustion underneath. It was release, not rest. Just a little escape but not healing.

Rest was never something they earned. It was something they bypassed entirely. Watching them taught me more than any conversation ever could. Being needed was safer than being known. Motion was proof of worth. Stillness meant you were not doing enough.

No one sat me down and said, "your value is conditional, love must be earned, rest is selfish." But I absorbed it anyway. I saw it in the way people praised them for their strength while overlooking their depletion. I felt it in the way the house relaxed when they held everything together. And somewhere along the way, I learned that pain was something you handled alone, that asking for help meant burdening people, and struggling meant you were not strong enough.

I wore independence like armor, convinced I was being strong, not realizing I was repeating a script written generations before I was born.

There is a moment in every therapist's office when a client says something that hits differently than they intended. Halfway through telling me about their childhood, their family, their habits, something stops them mid-sentence. Their expression shifts. A quiet, almost involuntary "oh" escapes. That is the moment they see the pattern for the first time, not as isolated choices or personal failures, but as something handed down. An inheritance they did not ask for but received anyway.

I had that moment, too; a therapist who needed a therapist. Sitting on a tan couch in my own therapist's office, deep into a session where I was explaining, again, why I could not ask for help even when I desperately needed it, why rest felt like failure, and why I measured my worth by how much I could carry without breaking. I was talking fast, the way I always did when I was defending something I did not want to examine too closely.

She let me finish. Then she asked one question, "Where did you learn that?"

I went silent.

That silence was not about searching for an answer. It was about realizing the question had cracked something open. I sank back into that same office, deep in my thoughts, tracing the pattern backward. Where did I learn that rest was selfish, that asking for help was burdening people, that my worth was tied to how much I could handle?

And then it hit me.

The answer did not come from a book or a single bad experience. It came from watching the women who raised me, from a family system where survival meant motion, love meant labor, and being needed was the only guaranteed form of belonging. I absorbed it so young and so deeply, I did not even know it was happening.

The realization was not comforting. It was heavy. Because if I had inherited this, if it had been passed down like hair texture or the shape of my hands, then I had been fighting the wrong battle. Not failing at life, but loyal to a story I never chose.

I sat in my car after that session and cried, not the releasing kind but the kind that comes from finally understanding something you cannot un-know. My whole body needed a moment to catch up to what my mind had just accepted. Something in me went still.

The parking lot was ordinary. Other people moved through it like nothing had happened, a woman loading groceries, a man on his phone, the world continuing its business while I sat there unraveling in the most invisible way possible. I do not know how long I stayed there. Long enough for the crying to stop, long enough for something to settle into a stillness I could finally name. I kept thinking about my mother's voice on the phone, my grandmother moving through that house, and how I had spent years trying to prove I was different, only to realize I had been repeating the exact same pattern with better lighting. The inheritance was not a choice, but keeping it was.

I called my mother that night. She has called me Ree for as long as I can remember. I did not know what I was going to say, just needed to hear her voice again, this time listening for something different. When she answered, I asked her something I had never asked before. "When is the last time you rested without feeling guilty about it?"

The pause that followed was long enough for me to know the answer.

"I do not know, Ree," she said finally. "I guess I never thought about it like that."

The phone stayed at my ear. I did not want to fill the space with words, just wanted to sit in it with her, in the honesty of it. Two women on a phone who had both been running on empty for so long we had stopped noticing the tank was low. She had given everything she had and then found more to give, and I had watched her do it, called it strength, and learned to do the same.

"I love you," I told her before we hung up.

She said it back the way she always does. Effortless. The easiest truth in the world.

It took me a long time to understand that love was never the problem. It was the price we believed love required.

The exhaustion I was carrying was not a personal failing. It was a family heirloom. One I did not have to keep.

Something changed in me after that session. I started noticing the script as it played: saying yes when I meant no, pushing through when my body was asking me to stop, measuring my worth by output instead of humanity. I started putting things down, quiet decisions that felt enormous. Saying no to requests that would have stretched me too thin. Asking for help without apologizing for needing it. I began seeing I had been carrying weight that was not mine, weight I accepted because that is what I had been taught. The question changed.

Not "Can I handle this?" but "Is this mine to carry?"

That is what inheritance means. You do not just get the patterns, you get the stories about what those patterns mean, the beliefs about what is required to be loved, the rules about who deserves rest and who must keep moving. And you carry those stories until someone asks you the question that cracks it all open, "Where did you learn that?"

On that tan couch, when my therapist asked where I learned exhaustion was the cost of love, I finally had an answer. The answer set me free, not because it was easy, but because it was true. The weight I had been carrying was not mine, and the script I had been following was not written for me. Once I could see that, I could start choosing a different story.

Not the one that said I had to earn rest by being useful, but the one that said I was already enough just by being here, the one that said peace was not something to perform but something to practice. And that practice begins with one simple, radical act: identifying what belongs to you and what does not.

The story ends the moment you decide it was never yours to carry.

Your Turn

You did not come up with this pattern on your own. You learned it, and you learned it early. These questions are asking you to trace it back, not to assign fault, but to understand what you have been carrying that was never actually yours. The weight feels familiar because you have held it your whole life. Familiar does not mean it belongs to you.

1. Think about the person who raised you or shaped you most. What did they never let themselves have? Rest? Help? Softness? Now look at your life. What are you repeating?

2. Write down something you do that you hate doing, but you keep doing it anyway. Now ask: Who taught me this was necessary? What would happen if I stopped?

3. Complete this sentence: I learned early that love meant ________. Then write, and because of that, I have been ________.

4. What belief about rest, work, or worth did you inherit that you have never questioned until now? Write it down. Then ask: Is this actually true, or is this just what I was taught?

5. If you could go back and tell the women who raised you one thing they did not know, what would it be? Now ask yourself: Am I living that truth or am I still carrying their patterns?

Chapter 5

The Body That Forgot How to Stop

Most people think rest is the absence of work. It is not. Rest is the presence of safety. I know this because I spent years confusing the two. And for many of us, safety has never felt accessible without motion. When you have been trained to associate stillness with threat, your body does not register peace as relief. It registers it as danger.

I used to think I was bad at resting because I lacked discipline, but the truth was more uncomfortable than that. I did not know what rest felt like. Depletion was familiar, and so was the performance of calm, the thin version of rest that happens between obligations. But actual rest, the kind that restores rather than pauses survival, was foreign. My body did not trust it. When the body does not trust stillness, silence is filled with noise: scrolling, planning, cleaning, anything to avoid the discomfort of being still.

The first time I chose to rest on purpose it was not a revelation. Chris was at after-school care, and I had an extra hour before pickup. The old version of me would have filled it immediately with emails, laundry, something productive to justify the time. Instead, I lay on the couch in the quiet and closed my eyes. The guilt showed up right on schedule: he is waiting for you; you should be doing something. But I stayed there anyway. At some point, I heard birds outside on the balcony and opened my eyes. Two hummingbirds were hovering near the tree just outside my window. I had walked past that window a hundred times and never noticed them. They had probably been there all along, just waiting for me to be still enough to see them. When I picked Chris up, he was fine and happy. The world had not fallen apart because I rested, and nothing had been lost. I had just been so convinced something would be that I had never tested it.

There is a difference between pausing and resting. Pausing is what happens when you run out of options. Resting is what happens when you feel safe enough to stop. The body knows the difference and does not relax during a pause. Instead, it stays alert, waiting for the next demand. Real rest requires the nervous system to believe that stillness will not cost you your safety. For those of us who learned early that being useful kept us loved, that belief does not come naturally.

The difference shows up in ways most people never name. During a pause, the mind stays on-call, mentally cycling through the list, waiting for the next demand. The break is happening, but you are not inside it. Rest requires something more honest: putting the list down completely, not delaying it but releasing it, until nothing is waiting, nothing is required, and you are not available to anything except yourself. Most of us pause thousands of times a day. Many of us have never truly rested.

I started noticing how my body moved through the day, even when nothing demanding was happening. I would wake up already calculating before my feet hit the floor, my mind racing before the first cup of coffee. I would sit down to eat breakfast but never settle into the chair, perched on the edge, mentally running through what came next. By evening my neck was tight without knowing why, my mind was still scanning for what I had forgotten or what might go wrong. By the end of the day, exhausted even though nothing visible had demanded it. The body had been working the entire time, just not at anything anyone could see.

That is what happens when rest becomes a performance instead of a state. You go through the motions, sitting, lying down, taking a break, but the system never actually settles. You are resting in posture but not in nervous system.

When I first tried resting intentionally, I felt guilty. Not the rational kind of guilt that comes from neglecting something important, but the existential kind that whispers, who are you if you are not doing something? That question lived in my chest like a stone. I would sit down to rest and immediately think of three things I should be doing instead, my mind spiraling down the same loop. *If I am not moving, I fall behind. If I am not producing, I am wasting time. If I am not useful, I am not enough.*

It took me longer than I wanted to admit before I realized my exhaustion had become my language. When people asked how I was, I said tired. When I wanted connection, I bonded over busyness. When I felt proud, it was because I had endured something difficult.

The realization of my level of exhaustion hit during a routine check-in with a colleague. She asked how my weekend was, and I immediately launched into everything I had accomplished: cleaned the apartment, meal prepped, caught up on emails, squeezed in a workout. She smiled and said, "That sounds exhausting. Did you enjoy any of it?" I opened my mouth to answer and realized I did not know. The weekend had happened and I had not been paying attention to how I felt. I had been tracking what I had done.

What she said did not leave me. I started taking note of how often I measured my days by productivity instead of presence. I used exhaustion as evidence I was living fully. Being busy made me feel important, and rest made me feel guilty. Somewhere along the way, I had confused exhaustion with identity.

If I was not tired, I did not know who I was.

The cost of that confusion was steep.

I became someone who could function endlessly but could not feel joy without earning it first.

The change did not come from deciding to rest more. It came from learning to tolerate the discomfort of stillness. I started small: five minutes of sitting without reaching for my phone, a walk without a destination, eating a meal slowly without distraction. At first, it felt wrong, like breaking a rule I had never agreed to but somehow always followed.

Sitting in peace felt like wasting time, like something bad was about to happen and I was unprepared because I was not moving. The guilt arrived immediately: you should be answering that email, you should be cleaning, you should be doing something productive. My mind raced through the to-do list while I sat there doing nothing. I would feel selfish for taking up space without earning it through labor. Even five minutes of sitting still felt like breaking an unspoken rule.

The body resisted and the mind filled the space with urgency, but I stayed with it. I practiced feeling the discomfort without fixing it. Over time the noise faded.

There were setbacks. One Saturday I cleared my entire day with no plans, no obligations, nothing required of me. I thought it would feel like relief. Instead, I spent the morning pacing the apartment, picking up my phone every few minutes, looking for something to fix, organize, or respond to. By noon I felt worse than I had all week, irritable and restless, like I was wasting time in my own life. I ended up deep cleaning the kitchen to stop the agitation. The rest I had tried to give myself had backfired entirely.

That was when I realized my nervous system did not know what to do with space. It had been trained to function under pressure, to move through demands, to stay alert for the next thing that needed me. When nothing was required, my body interpreted that as danger, not relief. Rest was not the problem. The absence of urgency was the problem.

Of course it did that. Motion had kept me safe once. Being useful had kept me connected. Staying busy had prevented questions I was not ready to answer. My body learned stillness meant something bad was coming, that rest meant I was failing, that doing nothing meant I did not matter. It was not wrong to learn that. It was adapting to what my life required at the time, and the pattern worked until my life no longer required it.

Here is what I learned: you cannot rest your way into peace if your nervous system interprets rest as abandonment. The work is not about forcing yourself to slow down. It is about teaching your body that slowing down will not cost you your worth, that safety does not depend on your capacity, and that love is not conditional on your usefulness. These are not beliefs you adopt through logic. They are patterns you rewire through practice.

There is a difference between performing wellness and practicing it.

Performing wellness looks like self-care that exhausts you: the face mask while you answer emails, the yoga class you rush to after a twelve-hour day, the meditation app you feel guilty for not using, the hair appointment and nail appointment squeezed between obligations. It is rest as another task to complete, one more way to prove you are trying hard enough.

Practicing wellness is different. It means choosing the nap over the face mask, saying no to the yoga class because your body needs actual rest and not structured movement, deleting the meditation app because the notifications stress you out more than the practice helps. It means listening to what your body needs in that moment, not what you think it needs. Rest without performance, stillness without apology, and peace without having to look peaceful.

For some, the work is learning to say no without guilt, for others it is sitting without distraction, and for me it was noticing when I reached for busyness to avoid feeling. I started tracking the moments when rest felt threatening. What was I afraid would happen if I stopped? The answer was always the same: I would be forgotten, dismissed, or seen as less valuable.

Those fears did not disappear but naming them loosened their grip.

Resting is not a reward you earn. It is a practice you return to repeatedly until your body begins to trust it. That trust does not happen overnight. It builds in small, consistent moments where you choose stillness over motion, presence over performance, and peace over productivity.

You will resist it at first. That is normal. Your nervous system is doing what it was trained to do, and what it was trained to do is protect you. The work is teaching that rest is not a threat, that sitting still is not the same as giving up, and that peace is not something you have to deserve.

Rest is not passive but an act of defiance in a world that profits from your depletion. Learning to rest well is one of the most radical things you can do, not because it is easy, but because it reclaims something the world taught you to give away: the belief that your worth is not tied to your output.

You are allowed to stop. You just had to learn to believe it.

Your Turn

Before you answer anything, take one slow breath and notice where you are holding tension right now. That is your starting point. These questions are not asking you to change your relationship with rest overnight. They are asking you to get honest about what rest has come to mean to you, and what your body does when you try to stop.

1. Think about a time you tried to sit still, still, no phone, no task, nothing. What did your body do? What did your mind do? How long did you last before reaching for a distraction? Write what happened.

2. Think about the last time you tried to rest. What did you tell yourself you should be doing instead? Whose voice was that? Where did you learn stillness means you are wasting time?

3. What does your nervous system think will happen if you stop moving? Write down the fear underneath the busyness. Be specific.

4. Describe what doing nothing would look like for you. Not a spa day or a vacation. Just an ordinary afternoon where you had no obligations or guilt. Can you even picture it?

5. Complete this sentence: I do not let myself rest because deep down, I believe that if I stop...

Chapter 6
The Day You Get Honest

Chris was staying with family. The apartment had gone quiet in the way it does when everything familiar has been set aside. I had dropped everything to be there, my home, my routines, the rhythm I knew. And that night I finally stopped pretending I did not feel what I had been feeling for months. I already knew the answer before I asked the question.

"Is this what you want?"

I needed clarity, needed him to tell me the truth so I could stop guessing, stop managing the tension in the air, stop pretending I did not feel the distance growing between us. He had been texting someone else. He told me about her, said it was nothing, and put the ring back on my finger. But when I asked that question, “Is this what you want?” he did not answer. He said communication was hard for him, that he did not know how to convey it. What he gave me was silence dressed as consideration.

I felt it in my body before I could name it.

That silence burned, not loud pain but something that does not announce itself, a low constant ache that sits with you in the morning and follows you through the day. I kept waiting for him to give me something to hold onto, some fragment of honesty to work with, but he never did. In that absence I realized something I was not ready to admit yet: I was asking the wrong person for permission to leave. The person I needed honesty from was not him. It was me.

That night, I did what I had always done. Pretended to be fine, laid down, closed my eyes, and told myself I was okay. But my body would not cooperate. There was a warmth moving through me, the kind that comes when something true is trying to get out and you keep pushing it back down. Sleep would not come. The room was dark and still, and everything was audible: the hum of the refrigerator, the sounds from outside, my own breathing, while my mind stayed completely awake. I turned the conversation repeatedly, unable to land anywhere. And somewhere in that restlessness something unexpected surfaced. Anger. Not at him, but at myself, for staying quiet so long, for asking a question I already knew the answer to, for needing him to confirm what I already felt.

Honesty always costs something before it gives anything back.

People love to imagine truth as a clean, bright exhale. They say, just be honest and you will feel better. Sometimes that is true. More often, honesty lands like guilt or uncertainty. Your throat closes before you speak. Your stomach twists after the words leave your lips. Honesty is rarely smooth. It peels back old paint to show what has been hiding underneath. It is raw and uncomfortable, but it is necessary. If it were easy, we would all live in it every day.

The first time you tell the truth, an alarm goes off internally. A voice insists you are ungrateful, selfish, or weak. That noise is not proof you are wrong but proof you are walking past an old rule. Many of us learned to confuse silence with loyalty and exhaustion with love. When honesty finally pushes through, guilt rises to drag us back toward what is familiar: the silence, the performance, the pretending everything is fine.

Think of guilt as a guard dog posted at the edge of your life. It barks to keep you from leaving the yard. The sound is loud, but the bite is never real. Guilt is noise, not truth. It took me years to realize the barking stops when you stop obeying it.

In that apartment, the guard dog was loud. I could hear every reason I should stay quiet; every excuse I could make for why his silence was okay. Maybe he was scared, maybe he needed time, maybe I was asking too much. But underneath all that noise was a calmer truth: I knew. I knew the relationship was not what I needed it to be, I knew I was holding onto a vision that no longer matched reality, and I knew if I stayed silent, I would spend the next decade managing his emotions while abandoning my own.

The problem was, I had stopped paying attention to myself a long time ago. I had learned to listen to everyone else's needs, everyone else's comfort, everyone else's version of what my life should look like. But my own voice, the one that spoke the truth in still moments, I had trained myself to ignore it. I called it overthinking. I called it being too sensitive. I called it anything but what it was: the sound of my intuition trying to save me.

That night in the apartment, there were no answers to leave with, only more questions. But something started that I had not done in years. I started listening.

Not to him. Not to the guilt. Not to the voice that said I should be grateful for what I had. I started listening to what my body had been signaling all along, the tension that arrived when he walked into the room, and the exhaustion that came from managing his mood while pretending mine did not matter.

That night, I stopped asking the wrong person. I stopped waiting for him to give me permission to feel what I was feeling, stopped asking him to validate my reality, and started asking myself instead: what do I need? What does honesty look like when no one else is in the room?

Self-honesty is when you stop spinning the story and admit what is real. The job that drains you, the relationship that looks fine from the outside but hollow from the inside. The goals that no longer fit who you are becoming. Pretending to yourself is the deepest exhaustion of all. You cannot rest if your truth keeps you awake, and you cannot recover if you refuse to name what is hurting you.

I started keeping voice memos. Late at night, when Chris was asleep and the house was quiet, I would sit on the edge of my bed and record what I was really feeling, not the version I told my friends or my family, not the story I wanted to be true, just the raw unfiltered truth. I am exhausted. I am angry. I do not think this is going to work. I do not know how to leave but I know I cannot stay.

The first time I listened back to one of those recordings, I cried. Not because it was sad, but because I finally heard myself, the voice I had been ignoring for years, the truth I had been too scared to name. And once I heard it, I could not unhear it.

But hearing myself did not make anything easier. It made everything harder. The truth sat there, undeniable, and I had no idea what to do with it. Admitting what I felt did not give me a map forward, only the confirmation that I was standing somewhere I could not stay. The clarity I had wanted so badly felt less like relief and more like being handed a problem with no solution.

About two weeks into recording those voice memos, I was getting ready for work and caught myself smiling at nothing. It was real, the kind that arrived without an audience. It startled me. I stood there in the bathroom, toothbrush in hand, trying to figure out what had changed.

I realized I had stopped lying to myself. That was it. The relief was not in having answers but in finally admitting I did not have them.

Uncertainty hurts less than pretending.

I wish I could say the work ended when I started listening. But learning to listen is a practice, not a destination. Even now, years later, I still catch myself dismissing my own truth, still catch myself asking for permission from people who do not have the right to grant it, still waiting for external validation instead of trusting what I already know.

But the difference is, I notice it now. I notice when I am talking myself out of what I feel. I notice when I am performing certainty to cover up doubt. I notice when I am listening to the noise instead of the truth. Noticing is where the power lives because once you see it, you can change paths.

Listening is not passive. It is one of the most active, demanding things you can do. When you truly listen to yourself, you must be willing to act on what you hear. Acting on your truth, especially when it disappoints people or disrupts the status quo, takes courage.

The guard dog still barks sometimes. The guilt still rises. The voices still tell you that you are wrong. But underneath all of that, there is a truth that has been patient enough to wait for you.

This is where the work begins. Not in the bold moment of walking away, but in the quiet moment when you finally stop ignoring yourself. When you record that first voice memo. When you admit to yourself, even if you cannot admit it to anyone else yet, that something is wrong. When you start paying attention to what your body has been trying to tell you all along.

You do not need all the answers. You do not need a plan. You do not need to know what comes next.

You have always known. You just needed permission to believe it.

Your Turn

Honesty rarely arrives as a clear, tidy revelation. It usually comes as a quiet knowing you have been working hard to avoid. These questions are making space for that knowing to land. You do not need to be ready. Being willing to stop talking yourself out of what you already sense is true is enough.

1. What is the truth you have been avoiding saying out loud, even to yourself? Not the polite version. Not the version that makes sense. The raw, unedited truth that scares you because once you say it, it can't be unsaid.

2. Think about the last time you felt that burning sensation in your stomach, the one that tells you something is wrong. What were you doing? Who were you with? What did you do with that feeling? Did you listen or did you talk yourself out of it?

3. Write like you are talking out loud. Start with: *If I am being completely honest with myself...* Do not stop until you have said the thing you have been avoiding. Or record a voice memo if that feels easier.

4. What are you pretending not to know about your

relationship, your job, your life, yourself? What truth are you managing around instead of facing directly?

5. Complete this sentence: I have been waiting for permission to feel this, but the truth is...

Part Three
The Practice

"As a Black Woman, I define self-care as the ability to safely and comfortably exhale."

- Bethanee Epifani J. Bryant

Chapter 7

Your Body Did Not Get the Memo

She walked into my office the way most of my clients do in that first session, moving like her body did not believe sitting counted. Her name was Aisha. She was a project manager at a tech startup, the person everyone called when things went sideways because she always figured it out. No kids. Dating someone she was not sure about. Her hands moved before the rest of her body did, adjusting her bag, smoothing her blouse, reaching for the arm of the chair twice before she sat down. Even after she settled her leg kept bouncing, small quick movements, while everything in her was already scanning for the next thing.

"I set the boundary," she said, the words coming out tight, almost defensive, like she was arguing with someone who was not in the room. *"I told my boss I would not answer emails after six anymore. I told my sister I could not keep taking her kids every weekend because I have my own life. I even told my mother I needed space and could not do Sunday dinners for a while. I did the work you are supposed to do. So why do I feel like this?"*

Her hands kept moving as she spoke, picking at her cuticle, adjusting her hair, reaching for the water bottle she never drank from. She had drawn lines around her time, her energy, and her availability. But her body had not received the news.

This is what most people do not understand about boundaries. The decision is only the beginning. You can tell people no and your body can still be on high alert. You hang up the phone and something in you is still bracing, still waiting for the consequence that never comes, still scanning for the fallout. Your words changed but your nervous system did not get the memo yet. And that gap, between the decision you made and the safety your body has not learned to feel, is exactly where the real work lives.

Most of us were never taught how to pause. Nobody sat us down and explained how to listen to the body, how to notice when capacity is reached, how to choose yourself without feeling disloyal. What we were shown instead was performance. Being agreeable was rewarded. Staying available was celebrated. Holding emotions so other people did not have to deal with theirs was called being strong. Being strong was called being mature. Being mature was called being independent. All of those were rewards for learning how to override. None of them taught us how to pause.

Aisha was the oldest of three. Excellence was expected, not celebrated. Struggle was weakness. Asking for help meant you were incapable. She managed her younger siblings' schedules, sensed tension before it surfaced, and smoothed it over before anyone noticed. By the time she was twelve she had memorized the pattern: notice what people need, provide it before they ask, stay steady no matter what you feel. She carried that pattern into adulthood. At work, she was the person who could handle anything. In her relationship, she adapted and made it easy. With her family, she was the steady one who showed up. She had started setting boundaries, but her body had not caught up.

Years before I sat across from Aisha, I had been the one in that chair. I had set boundaries with my family, at work, with the people who had learned to expect my yes. I had done the external work. But my mind would spin through worst-case scenarios when my phone rang. My body would brace every time I heard a certain tone in someone's voice. I had changed what I was available for, but not what my system expected.

This is what the override pattern does. It runs in the background long after you have made the conscious decision to stop. When the body lives in constant alert mode for too long, it stops recognizing the difference between an actual threat and ordinary stress. Everything gets treated as urgent. It shows up as irritability, as rushing, as words spilling out faster than intended, as a mind looping through the same thought three times before you realize it, as urgency attached to things that aren't emergencies. Even when the day is over, you cannot land. For some people, it goes in the other direction and the system does not speed up, it shuts down. You are doing things, but you do not feel connected. You forget what you ate. You start resenting everyone. You are there but not present. Both versions look like they are functioning. Neither is regulated.

Pausing is not a concept. It is a physiological intervention. Your body has been doing exactly what you taught it to do. You showed it that pushing through was strength, that ignoring what you felt was loyalty, and that stopping meant you were not enough. It believed you. Now you are asking it to learn something different, and that does not happen overnight. It happens one pause at a time. Every time you stop instead of overriding, you send your body a new message: I hear you, you are safe, and you do not have to keep pushing to get my attention.

The sequence is simple enough to remember and real enough to use.

First, notice. Not hours later when you are replaying everything, but right when it starts. Catch the first signal. For many people, it shows up as restlessness, hands that cannot stay still, scanning the room without meaning to. For others it is physical, a drop in the stomach, heat rising, a flush. Some people notice their breath gets shallow. Others do not feel more, they feel less. They go foggy or flat, words trailing off mid-sentence. That is not fine. That is the system moving toward shutdown to conserve. Those are the ones to catch quickly. Aisha's signals were her stomach and her hands. Your signals will repeat themselves. Write them down so you remember them.

Second, name it. Once you put words to what is happening, it no longer swallows you. You narrate your own experience: I am in go mode. My body is bracing. I am trying to fix something. I am starting to shut down. I am overriding what I feel. That is not being dramatic. That is taking leadership over your internal experience instead of letting old patterns choose for you.

Third, regulate. This is where people try to make it complicated. It does not have to be. You need to send your body one clear message of safety. Breathe with a longer exhale than inhale, which tells the body it can leave fight or flight. Orient yourself by looking around and naming what you see and hear, so your brain understands you are here right now and not in an old situation. Or use contact, hand on your ribs, hand on the back of your neck, both feet pressed into the floor. Steady pressure tells the body it is present and safe.

Fourth, decide. Not before you regulate. When the system is activated, every decision feels urgent. When you pause and regulate first, you get your discernment back. You can ask yourself what you need right now, not what will make the feeling stop fastest, not what will keep everyone else comfortable. What do you need?

Here is what that looks like in practice. You just told your mother you are not driving across town every weekend because it is too much right now, closed the conversation, and got off the phone. Most people think the work is finished there. What happens next is where the growth lives. Your mind starts rehearsing an apology, replaying the conversation to make sure you were not too harsh, worrying about whether she is upset, reaching for your laptop or your phone even though you are exhausted. All of that is your system trying to escape the discomfort of having chosen yourself.

This is where you pause. Not to punish yourself. Not to obsess. To regulate. To remind your body that disappointment is not danger and that no one is coming for you because you said no. A pause might look like running warm water over your hands and standing there breathing. It might look like sitting with both feet on the floor and naming out loud everything you see in the room, returning your brain to present time. It might look like placing your hand on your ribs and saying aloud: I made a good choice. I can feel the discomfort and keep the boundary. I am not in danger. Those words matter because the body believes what it is told repeatedly.

People do not end up depleted because of one large moment. It is the email answered at ten at night to prove you are still reliable. It is telling your body five more minutes but meaning thirty. None of that looks serious in the moment. Together it keeps the system on high. The pause interrupts that pattern before it accumulates.

Two weeks passed. Aisha came back looking different. Not lighter exactly. Steadier. She sat down and there was less movement. Her hands rested in her lap.

"Something happened," she said. For the first time, since I met her, her voice was calm.

"Tell me."

"My sister called. Last minute. She needed me to watch the kids because her sitter canceled and she had this work thing she could not miss. And immediately my stomach dropped, that falling feeling came. I felt my hands start to move, reaching for my keys, getting ready to say yes. But I caught it. I noticed it. I said it out loud: my body is bracing. I am about to override."

She paused, and I watched her remember it. "I put the phone down. I pressed my feet into the floor. I did the breathing, the exhale longer. And I just sat there for a minute. Then I texted her back and replied, "I cannot today, but I can help this weekend if that still works."

She looked at me like she was waiting to be told she had done something wrong.

"And?" I asked.

"She said okay and figured it out. And I did not spiral. I did not replay the conversation for three hours. I did not check my phone every five minutes to see if she was mad. I just moved on. I made dinner. I watched a show. I went to bed. And the next morning I woke up and I felt lighter. Like something had released."

That is what regulation does. It does not erase discomfort. It shortens the distance between the trigger and the return to center. It teaches the body that a boundary does not mean danger. It teaches the system that stopping is allowed and that choosing yourself does not cost you your safety.

"I did not realize how much energy I was spending just trying to manage everyone's feelings," she said. "All the time. Even when no one was asking me to."

The override pattern runs in the background. You do not notice it until you start interrupting it.

There will be days when you forget. Days when the old urgency grabs you and you are halfway through the spiral before you realize what happened. Forgetting is not failure. It is part of being human. The work is not about perfection. It is about return. Every time you notice it, every time you name it, every time you regulate and decide from steadiness instead of panic, you are teaching your body a different response.

Aisha taught me that this work is not about becoming someone who never feels the override impulse. It is about becoming someone who knows how to interrupt it. Someone who can catch the signal, name it, and choose differently.

That is what pausing really means. You stop long enough to let your nervous system catch up to your life. You practice regulation until it becomes rhythm.

One pause at a time.

Your Turn

The decision and the nervous system are two entirely different things. You can know exactly what to do and still feel every impulse firing against it. These questions are not asking you to judge that. They are asking you to get curious about it. Your body is not working against you. It is protecting you with everything it learned to do a long time ago. These questions help you look at what it learned.

1. Think about the last time someone asked you for something and your stomach dropped, but you said yes anyway. What did your body do in that moment? What signal did you ignore? Write down exactly what happened before you overrode yourself.

2. Finish this sentence: The last time I paused to ask myself what I actually needed, I... If you cannot finish it, that is your answer. Write about why stopping feels impossible.

3. Pull out your phone right now. Look at your texts and emails from the last 48 hours. How many times did you respond immediately even though you did not want to? How many times did you feel the urge to say no but typed yes? Count them, then ask yourself why.

4. Your body has been trying to tell you something for weeks, or months, or years. What is it? The thing you keep pushing through, explaining away, calling dramatic, or promising you will deal with later. Write it down. Do not soften it.

5. Here is the hard one. If you paused before reacting for one full week, if you noticed, named, regulated, and then decided, what would have to change in your life? Who would be disappointed? What would you lose? Be specific. Then ask yourself, is that loss worth more than the cost of ignoring yourself?

Chapter 8
A Boundary Is Not a Wall

Knowing what to do and doing it are two different things.

I will never forget my phone ringing while I was in the middle of writing up a client's notes. A family member, third call that day. I watched it vibrate across my desk, her name flashing on the screen. I noticed what my body wanted to do. I chose something different.

The old me would have answered on the first ring, dropped everything, absorbed whatever she was carrying and held it until she felt better. That is what I have always done, what good family members do, I thought.

We had already been texting. The conversation was happening; I was present and engaged. But the calls kept coming because a text was not enough for what she needed that day. She wanted a voice. She wanted real time. And the old version of me would have given it without a second thought, dropped the notes, absorbed whatever she was carrying, and held it until she felt better. That is what I have always done, what good family members do, I thought.

But I was in the middle of something that required my full attention. I let it go to voicemail, finished my notes, and texted back an hour later. I replied, "I cannot talk now, but I can call you tomorrow afternoon. Does that work?"

The response came fast, "Never mind. I will figure it out."

The guilt arrived immediately. *You are being selfish. She needed you. What if it was important?*

But I did not call back. I sat with the discomfort. Let my body feel what it needed to feel without acting on it. Reminded myself her disappointment was not my emergency.

I had been learning something. For a long time, I thought boundaries were supposed to feel like relief, like a door closing on the noise, like finally exhaling. But the first time I held one, I felt guilty and small, like I had failed someone who needed me. That is not what the books told me it would feel like. Nobody warned me that doing the right thing for yourself could feel so much like doing something wrong. Boundaries are not rejection. They are how you soothe yourself when the world will not stop asking. Your body does not know that yet, but it can learn.

Later that week, I sat across from Maya in my office. She had her phone face down on the table between us, but she kept glancing at it.

She had started therapy because she was drained. When I asked her what she needed, she said the same thing most of my clients say in that first session.

"I don't know. I just need to figure out how to do it all without losing my mind."

She glanced at her phone again, then forced her eyes back to me.

"My daughters," she said. "They are with their dad this week but they text constantly. Not because something is wrong.

Because they have never had to wait for me. Every question, every decision, every moment of discomfort finds its way to my phone first. I have become their first line of defense against feeling anything uncomfortable. Riley just sends screenshots. Of conversations. With her friends. With their dad. Like I am supposed to decode them and tell her what to do."

She laughed but it came out sharp. "I know I should just put the phone away. But what if it is an emergency?"

"How often is it an emergency?" I asked.

"Never." She said it fast, definitive. "But I cannot stop checking."

This is where most people get stuck. They think the work is behavioral: saying no, creating distance, protecting time. But Maya had already tried that. She had already tried putting the phone down. The impulse kept returning anyway because her body was still running the old program, even when her mind had decided to change. Setting a boundary is not a decision. It is practice. And the practice must include the nervous system, or it will not hold.

Honesty opens the door, but boundaries keep it from swinging shut. You can speak the truest words of your life, but without limits to protect them, those truths dissolve the moment someone leans on you. Honesty says, this is what I need. Boundaries are the structure that keeps that truth alive when the test comes.

Most of us never learned how to build that structure. We were taught how to stay agreeable, not truthful. We were rewarded for being dependable, not for being discerning. We learned to anticipate needs before they were spoken, to sense tension before it surfaced, to manage everyone's emotions while suppressing our own.

When you live in that pattern long enough, the body adapts to it. Peace becomes equated with pleasing, and the belief sets in that staying useful, polite, and flexible protects you from conflict, disappointment, or loss. But boundaries are not a luxury for people who have time. They are a necessity for people who have survived.

"What happens when you do not respond right away?" I asked Maya.

She moved in her seat, picking at the edge of her cardigan button. "They get upset. They say I am not being supportive. Or they will text more. Sometimes they will call their dad and complain that I am ignoring them, and then he will text me asking what is wrong."

"And how does that feel in your body?"

She closed her eyes. "Like I am failing. Like I am a bad mom. My throat closes. My hands go numb. I feel like I have to fix it immediately or everything will fall apart."

“So responding is not about them needing you," I said. "It is about you needing to not feel that way."

She opened her eyes and looked at me. "I never considered it from that angle."

“What do I do?" Maya asked. "Just stop responding?"

"No," I said. "You decide what feels sustainable. And then you practice it. Consistently."

We worked on it together. The boundary was simple: check the phone at three set times during the day when her daughters were with their dad, morning, afternoon, and evening. The rest of the time the phone stayed on Do Not Disturb. She told her daughters the plan and explained that in case of a true emergency they could call their dad or 911, but for everything else she would respond at her designated times. They resisted. They complained. They tested it. But she held the line.

The first week was hard. She felt the pull every time her phone was silent, the fear that something terrible would happen and she would not know. But nothing terrible happened. Her daughters adapted. They learned their questions could wait, that not every feeling required her immediate attention, that they could sit with discomfort for a few hours. That one boundary gave Maya something she had not had in years: space that belonged only to her.

She came back two weeks later, and I noticed something was different before she even sat down. Her shoulders were relaxed. Softer. She did not reach for her phone when she settled into the chair. When she spoke, her voice was steadier.

"Something happened," she said, and there was a slight smile at the edge of it.

"Tell me."

"I read a book." She said it like she was confessing to something. "For an hour. Uninterrupted. I did not check my phone once."

I waited.

"Mia texted me four times while I was reading. I could see the phone lighting up on the table next to me. And normally, I would have grabbed it. I would have stopped mid-sentence to see what she needed. But I did not. I just kept reading.

And when I finally picked up the phone an hour later, it was fine. She had figured it out on her own. The world did not end."

She looked at me, and this time the smile broke through. "I forgot I could do that. Just sit and read without being on-call for everyone."

"How did it feel?"

She exhaled, long and slow. "I did not realize how much energy I was spending just being available. Like, all the time. Even when no one was asking. It was like I could finally breathe."

I let that land before I said anything else.

"That is what boundaries do," I said. "They do not just protect your time. They protect your nervous system. They give you space to regulate. They let you stay in the calm you worked so hard to find."

The dynamic looked like motherhood in Maya's case. In yours, it may look completely different. The pattern underneath it is the same.

A boundary is a limit with a purpose. Not about control or distance but about clarity. A decision that protects your energy, your attention, and your peace. The real difference between hoping people will respect you and choosing to respect yourself. And that decision does not need to be loud. Boundaries are not built in confrontation. They are built in consistency. They sound like small sentences followed by steady action: I am not available right now. I can help for an hour, not the entire day. I do not take calls after eight. It is not what you say once that changes your life. It is what you keep honoring, even when it is uncomfortable.

A boundary is not always born from confrontation. Some of the clearest ones begin in silence.

One of my clients was a woman in her early forties who had spent fifteen years in a marriage that looked stable from the outside. She put it perfectly. "We do not fight. We are good parents. We have dinner together every night. But I feel like I am performing a role in someone else's play."

I asked her what her body did when he walked in the room. She paused. "My shoulders go up. My jaw tightens. I start mentally running through everything I need to manage so the evening goes smoothly."

"And when you are alone?"

"I can breathe."

That is the signal. The body knows before the mind catches up. The tension that arrives when certain people walk in the room, the way something in you starts bracing before a word is spoken, those are not random reactions. They are information. The body already knows what the mind is still negotiating. When you stop dismissing those signals and start paying attention, something becomes possible that was not before. You are no longer at war with yourself. You are finally on the same side.

I worked with a client once who described herself as the person everyone called first. Not because she was the most available. Because she had never once said she was not.

She was in a season when she had nothing left. She described sitting in her car after work one evening, phone in hand, already exhausted before she even walked through her front door. A close friend called in a moment of real pain and genuine need, but my client was already at capacity. She texted back instead of calling and said she needed until the next day. Her friend went quiet. Then distant.

My client came into session convinced she had done something wrong, that choosing herself had broken something that mattered.

The boundary had not broken the friendship. It had revealed it. What it exposed was the relationship had been built on her always being available. Her friend had not done anything wrong either, she had simply never been asked to wait before. The relationship survived, but it had to become something more honest and more mutual first. That is what boundaries do to relationships. They show you what was there.

There is a difference between a boundary and a wall. A wall isolates, built from resentment and years of silence and exhaustion, shutting everyone out. A boundary moves with intention, letting care in and keeping chaos out, allowing love to breathe instead of suffocating.

Boundaries will change your relationships. Some people will welcome them, exhaling when you finally say no because they had been waiting for you to stop performing. They will meet your honesty with their own, and the relationship will deepen in ways that were never possible when you were losing yourself inside it.

Others will resist. The ones who relied on your exhaustion will call it selfishness. They will say you have changed. They are right. You are no longer available to be managed, overextended, or silently resented for giving too much. That disruption is uncomfortable, but it is also information. Relationships that cannot survive your boundaries were never really built on love. They were built on your compliance.

And some will fall away entirely. That loss is real and worth grieving honestly. But understand what you are grieving: not the relationship as it was, but the hope of what it could have been if both people had been free to show up honestly from the start.

Eventually, the work of setting boundaries becomes less about defense and more about design. You start shaping a life reflective of your values instead of your fears. Saying yes to every opportunity stop being necessary because you trust what is meant for you will not require self-betrayal. You no longer stretch yourself thin to prove your love because you have learned real love does not require constant draining. Choices begin coming from stability, not scarcity.

Maya's phone still lights up. Her daughters still text. Her ex-husband still has opinions. Work still demands more than she wants to give, but something has changed in how she meets all of it. The phone is no longer grabbed every time it buzzes. The panic that said she must fix everything immediately no longer runs the room. She has learned she can care without carrying, that boundaries are not about pushing people away but about staying present for her own life.

This is how boundaries work in real life. They do not build walls but thresholds, places where you can stand and decide what enters and what does not, where peace is not something you hope for after everything is done but something you protect while the work is still happening.

The guilt fades. The world still makes its demands, but you meet them with clarity instead of panicking. The laptop closes when the day ends and you feel the difference between fatigue and fullness. The phone rings and you let it because silence is not loneliness. It is recovery. You rest, not because everything is finished, but because you finally believe you deserve to.

Boundaries are how you soothe yourself, not with bubble baths or forced gratitude, but with the steady decision to stop betraying yourself for the comfort of others.

Your Turn

A limit without self-understanding is just a rule you will keep finding reasons to break. These questions are asking you to look under the boundary, at what belief is driving it, what guilt keeps defending it, and what the relationship pattern has made it necessary in the first place. The hardest boundaries to name are usually the ones that matter most. Take your time.

1. What boundary have you been avoiding because setting it would mean admitting you have been giving too much for too long? Write it down. The real one. Not the one that sounds reasonable. The one that scares you.

2. What have you been calling love that is availability? What have you been calling loyalty that is exhaustion? Be specific about the relationship and be honest about the cost.

3. If the people in your life had to adjust to a version of you that was no longer always available, who would adapt and who would disappear? What does that answer tell you about what those relationships are built on?

4. Think about the last time you held a limit and guilt showed up immediately. What did you tell yourself in that moment? What did you do with it?

5. Is there a relationship in your life that only worked because you were always available? What happened or what do you think would happen if you stopped being the one who never said no?

Chapter 9

Setbacks Are Part of the Story

There are seasons when progress slips away without announcement. You simply look up one day and realize the momentum you fought for has slowed, the rhythm you worked so hard to build feels distant, and the practices that used to ground you feel like another obligation. You cannot remember the exact moment it started slipping.

For me, that moment came during a stretch when my health was supposed to be improving. I had been consistent, focused, and disciplined. My body was stronger than it had been in years, my habits were aligned, I was eating better, moving more, sleeping according to something resembling a schedule. I felt like I had finally found a rhythm reflecting the care I had been trying to give myself since I first sat on that tan couch and admitted I was disappearing.

Then life began to move faster than I could keep up with.

The emotional weight of work grew heavier. My practice was expanding with new clients and more responsibility, and my son needed me in different ways as he got older. Logistics became more complex with school schedules, activities, and co-parenting negotiations that required more energy than I had to give. Without realizing it, I moved from being in my body to treating my body like another deliverable.

The health progress I had built did not vanish overnight. It dissolved under the weight of everything else that needed me.

There was no single moment of clarity, just a gradual numbness settling where awareness used to be. I stopped feeling proud of my progress and started feeling nothing about it at all. That was the signal I overlooked: not the skipped workouts, but the disappearance of the feeling that made them matter.

I stopped going to the gym—not all at once. I started missing a day here and there, then a week, then two. I told myself I was tired, that I would get back to it, that it was just a busy season. Meal planning fell away next. Whatever was convenient became the standard. Breakfast disappeared because there was no time, and lunch happened standing at my desk because sitting felt like wasting minutes. I stopped checking in with myself, stopped asking what I needed, and just kept moving.

The hardest part was not starting over. It was the anger that arrived with it, disappointment turning into a language you speak to yourself when no one else is listening, the voice saying you should have known better on repeat until you believe it.

The anger had layers. I was mad at myself for slipping, mad that after all the work, all the therapy, all the voice memos and boundaries and pauses, I could still end up here. And underneath that anger was the thing I did not want to admit, I had believed that doing the work meant I would never have to start over again. That belief was the real problem.

Underneath that anger was grief, too, another layer that needed to be peeled back. I had confused consistency with control. When the control slipped, it felt like my identity did, too.

I stopped introducing myself as someone who prioritized her health. Stopped mentioning the routines I had built when people asked how I was doing. Stopped feeling like the version of me I had worked so hard to become. In her place was someone familiar, capable on the outside but running on empty on the inside.

I had built my sense of self around being the person who figured it out, the one who survived, who got up every time she fell, who kept going no matter what. That identity had served me. It got me through the hardest seasons of my life, but it also became a cage. Because if I was the person who always figured it out, then what did it mean when I could not? If I was the person who kept going, then what did it say about me when I needed to stop?

It happened on a Wednesday. I woke up at five in the morning like I always did. When I tried to sit up, pain shot through my back, not the dull ache I had been carrying for weeks but something sharp and electric, the kind that reminds you your body has been keeping score long after you stopped listening. I lay there, staring at the ceiling, telling myself it would pass, that I just needed to stretch, that I could push through.

I could not push through.

I managed to get out of bed, moving like someone twice my age, got my son ready for school, dropped him off, and came home to sit on the edge of my bed with my laptop open, trying to work through the pain, clients' notes, emails, slides to finish. Everything was blurring together and my body had stopped cooperating. For the first time in years, I could not function my way through it.

I called my doctor and made an appointment that afternoon. Sitting in the exam room while she asked questions I did not want to answer felt like being caught. "How long has this been happening? When did you last take a full day off? Are you sleeping? Eating? Moving?"

The answers were embarrassing. Months. Inconsistently. Barely at all.

She did not lecture me, just looked at me with the kind of knowing that made me want to cry. "Your body is telling you something," she said. "The question is whether you're going to listen before it gets louder."

I left with a referral for physical therapy and a prescription for muscle relaxers I did not fill. Medication was not what I needed. Stopping was. But stopping felt like giving up, like admitting failure, like proving I was not strong enough to handle my own life.

So, I drove back and laid down on the living room floor because the bed felt too far away. And I just stopped. Not because I wanted to, but because I had no choice left.

Weeks passed before I moved with intention again, not weeks of clarity or progress but weeks of small stillness, of letting my body rest without demanding anything from it. Until one Saturday morning something in me was ready.

We talk about bouncing back, as if that is the goal. As if resilience means you snap right back into place like nothing happened. But the bounce is what breaks you. What you need is not to bounce back but to land, to sit, to let yourself be exactly where you are without rushing to fix it.

True resilience is slower and steadier than people imagine. It means sitting in the middle of your setback and deciding you can start again without shaming the part of you that paused. It means choosing to rebuild without punishing yourself for falling apart, understanding that self-trust is not earned through perfection but built through returning to yourself repeatedly, even after you drift.

When I think of setbacks now, I no longer see them as punishments. They are checkpoints. The pause in my health journey was not failure. It was a forced return to honesty. If you have ever stood in that same space—angry at yourself for slipping, afraid you will never find your rhythm again—remember this: you are not back at the beginning. You are at a deeper layer of understanding.

Every time you circle back, you bring wisdom with you. You have learned what does not work, what overextension costs, what pushing through takes from you. The setback is not proof you have failed. It is proof you have lived. You are still here, and that means there is something left to learn, not something to fix.

For me, it started with choosing to show up for small things again: the walk instead of the workout, the journal entry instead of the checklist, the ten-minute stretch on the living room floor instead of the full routine I used to do.

There was no triumph in those choices, just a steady agreement with myself that I would not ignore my body because life got heavy. Some days the walk was five minutes. Some days the journal entry was one line. Some days I would just lie on the floor and breathe. The point was not the outcome but that I stopped abandoning myself every time things got hard.

The first walk happened on a Saturday morning. My son was at his dad's. The apartment was still; no deadlines, no obligations, nowhere to be. The empty space terrified me because without the motion, without the tasks, I had to sit with what I had been running from: the shame and the grief of realizing I had done it again, pushing myself past capacity while calling it discipline.

I laced up sneakers I had not worn in weeks and walked out the front door before I could talk myself out of it. Walking to the end of the block was the only goal, no set distance, no pace, just movement.

The first few steps hurt. Everything in my body resisted, but I kept walking, one foot in front of the other. The headphones stayed inside, the podcast skipped. It was just the sound of my breath and the low hum of the neighborhood waking up.

I noticed things I had not in months. A woman was sitting on her front steps with a cup of coffee, not looking at her phone. Just sitting. Watching the street wake up. She did not notice me. But I noticed her. For a second, I wondered about the last time I had done that. Just sat somewhere without purpose. A dog barked behind a fence. Someone's sprinkler was on, even though it was barely dawn, the water catching light in a way that made me stop and watch. The air smelled like jasmine and wet earth. My neighbor's roses were overgrown, spilling over the fence in a way that felt both wild and intentional. A set of trash bins had been left out at the curb. A cat sat on a porch railing, watching me pass with complete indifference.

I made it to the end of the block, then the next one, then the one after that, not because I was trying to go farther but because stopping felt harder than continuing. My body started remembering what this felt like: movement without pressure, open air without an agenda, the ease that comes when no one is watching and nothing is required.

Something in me had loosened without me forcing it, my breath deepening without any thought behind it. At some point, I realized I had been humming. The last time that had happened was too long ago to place.

I walked into my house, poured some water, and sat on the couch. For the first time in months, I did not immediately reach for my phone, my laptop, or the list of things I should be doing. I just sat, breathing, noticing I was still here, that my body had carried me even when I was not kind to it, that I could start again. Not with a plan, a program, or a promise to do better. Just with a walk and the willingness to show up.

The grip I had on everything began to release, not in one big surrender but just enough to remember what breathing without bracing felt like.

Recovery does not move forward. It circles. Stability sometimes hides in ordinary decisions: drinking water before coffee, stepping outside for ten minutes before checking your phone, eating a real meal sitting down, choosing to sleep over one more hour of productivity. None of it looks significant, but all of it is.

Showing up is different from striving. Striving is trying to get somewhere. Showing up is willing to start from exactly where you are. One is fueled by urgency — striving. The other is fueled by trust — showing up. I could be gentle and still move forward.

It took me longer than I wanted to admit understanding what had happened. One evening, a few weeks into those small choices, I was stretching on my living room floor, nothing special, just the same ten minutes I had been doing most days. In mid-stretch, I realized I was not counting, timing myself, or planning what came next. I was just there, present, breathing, moving without agenda.

That is when it clicked. The discipline I had built before the routines, schedules, the rigidity, had all been about control, about keeping chaos away, but about proving I was strong enough to never break down again. I had been using structure as armor instead of using it to care for myself. The setback did not take away my discipline. It revealed what my discipline had been: fear dressed up as dedication.

I used to believe peace meant never losing momentum again. Now I know it means trusting yourself enough to come back, honestly and without punishment, without making the return harder than the fall.

Surviving is staying in motion because stopping feels too dangerous. Sustaining is knowing you can be still and will be okay.

Your Turn

You are not back at the beginning. You are further into the work than you have ever been, at a layer you could not have reached before now. These questions are asking you to be honest about where you actually are, not what you expected at this point. That is the only place anything real can start.

1. Think about the last time you had momentum and lost it. What was the first thing you stopped doing? Was it a practice, a habit, or simply checking in with yourself? Write about what the slipping felt like before you named it.

2. What does your anger sound like when you fall back into old patterns? Write out the exact voice. The words it uses. Where did you learn to speak to yourself that way?

3. What is the difference between the version of you that is surviving and the version that is sustaining? Describe both. What does each one look like on an ordinary Tuesday?

4. What is one small thing you could show up for today that is not about productivity or output? Not a task.

Not a goal. Just something that says to your body, *I am still here and I am paying attention.*

5. What would it mean for you to return to yourself without punishment? What would that actually look like in your life this week?

Chapter 10

The Bliss Rhythm

You have been learning about the BLISS Rhythm piece by piece. Now let me show you how it moves together. After you know how to come back when you fall, after the practices are no longer something you are trying to remember but something your body does naturally, there is a moment that comes after the rebuilding.

It will not arrive the way you might expect. There is no single morning where everything suddenly makes sense. It is ordinary and almost forgettable. You realize you have gone a few days without the weight underneath everything, without needing something to be different than it is, without counting down to the next time you can stop.

This is what I call the BLISS Rhythm, not a high point or a finish line, but a steady, lived pulse that starts carrying you once you finally get out of your own way.

The first time I felt it, I did not even recognize it for what it was.

It was one of those warm Los Angeles days where the sun felt personal, like it was shining specifically on me. I had a massage scheduled, something I used to see as indulgent and cancel when life felt too full. That day I almost canceled again. There were emails to respond to, work to finish, slides to prep, and my calendar said I had an hour, but my mind said I did not have time to waste being still.

I went anyway. Not because I wanted to, but because I had learned the hard way that ignoring my body's requests always cost more than honoring them.

The massage room was warm. Sunlight stretched across the floor in long, soft lines. The faint scent of eucalyptus oil lingered in the air. I was face down on the table when my mind started racing. *What if Chris needs me? What if that client emails? Did I respond to that text?* My phone was in my bag across the room and part of me wanted to get up to check it, just to be sure and just in case.

But I stayed. The masseuse introduced herself, Stephanie. Soft-spoken and unhurried. She asked if I had any areas of tension. I almost laughed. Everything did, but I only said my shoulders and lower back.

When she started my massage, I felt how much I had been holding. Her hands found knots in my shoulders I did not even know were there. The pressure should have hurt but somehow felt like relief, like my body had been waiting for an invitation to let go and had finally received one.

My mind kept trying to pull me away, cycling through the to-do list, the presentation, the email I forgot to send. Stephanie's hands kept working, steady and patient, and slowly my breath deepened. My jaw unclenched. The space behind my eyes, which had been tight for weeks, softened.

"You can let go," Stephanie said softly, not as a command but as an invitation.

And something in me did. My muscles stopped guarding themselves. The checklist in my head faded into background noise. For the first time in months, nothing was being planned, replayed, or braced for. I was just there. Present. Breathing. Feeling the warmth of the table seep into my back. Noticing how much lighter my body felt when I stopped asking it to produce.

When the session ended, Stephanie left the room so I could get dressed. I sat up slowly, almost dizzy from relaxation. My body felt different, loose, like I had been carrying something heavy for so long I forgot the weight was there until I finally set it down.

When I left, nothing had changed and everything had. The air felt clearer. My body was not demanding anything. I got in my car, rolled the windows down, and headed to pick up my son from school. He climbed in with his backpack half open, smiling, talking fast about his day. I remember laughing. Really laughing, the unguarded kind that surprises you because you forgot what it felt like.

That was bliss, not something I had to chase on vacations or through accomplishments but something already waiting for me in the rhythm of a regular day.

That moment was mine. But the feeling underneath it is available to anyone who has ever paused long enough to realize they had been missing from their own life.

And yet here is what nobody tells you about feeling good: it can be terrifying.

For weeks after that massage, I kept waiting for the other shoe to drop. I would catch myself in a peaceful moment, reading on the couch, cooking dinner without rushing, laughing with my son, and this voice would whisper, "*Do not get used to this. This is temporary. You are letting your guard down and something bad is going to happen.*"

My body had been in survival mode for so long that calmness felt like a trap, like something was missing, like relaxing too much would cost me the edge that was keeping me safe.

Learning to stay in the good moments without sabotaging them became its own practice. I had to teach my body that feeling good was not a setup for disaster, that joy did not need to be earned or defended, and that I could exhale without everything crashing down.

For so long, I thought bliss had to be earned, that it lived on the other side of progress or achievement. I believed I had to escape my life to enjoy it.

That version of bliss was built on running. Relief, not restoration. A reward for surviving long enough to take a break. Even then it never lasted because I could not rest into it. My mind was already calculating when it would end and when I would have to go back to holding it all together again.

What I have learned is that real bliss does not come from escape. I used to think a vacation would fix it: book the trip, get away from the noise, come back restored. It helped sometimes, for a few days. But home always meant the same inbox, the same pace, the same patterns. The escape never addressed what was underneath, just gave me a break from it. There is a difference between relief and restoration. Relief is temporary and requires you to leave your life to feel better. Restoration changes how you live inside your life so you do not need to escape it.

That is what this book has been building toward. Not a checklist or a set of rules, but a practice for living inside your own life without having to abandon yourself to survive it.

This practice has a name. I call it BLISS. It is not about constant happiness or some elevated state you have to chase. It is about building a life where your baseline is regulated, where your nervous system is not always on high alert, and where you can move through hard moments without falling apart.

BLISS is not a destination. It is a practice made up of five movements that work together so you can stop performing your life and start living it.

Breathe before you react, before you say yes, before you spiral. Your breath is the most direct way to tell your nervous system you are safe in that moment.

Breathing before you react means noticing when your breath has gone shallow, when it is sitting high in your chest instead of dropping into your body. That tightness is your nervous system signaling it needs a moment. The practice is simple: let your exhale be longer than your inhale. That one adjustment tells your body it is safe to leave high alert.

I remember sitting in my car before a difficult conversation I had been avoiding for weeks. My breath was tight. Shallow. Sitting high in my chest like it forgot how to drop. My hands were on the steering wheel, and my mind was already three steps ahead, rehearsing what I would say, bracing for how it might go wrong. I sat there for two minutes before I went inside. Not meditating or doing anything special. Just breathing out longer than I breathed in. Letting my exhale be slower than my inhale. That was it. By the time I walked through the door, I was not calm. I was present, and being present was enough to have the conversation without it destroying me.

Listen to what your body is actually telling you, not what you think it should be saying or what you wish it was telling you, but what is true in that moment.

Your body speaks in sensations. Heaviness in your limbs. Restlessness in your hands. Flatness in your voice. These are not random. They are signals. Most of us were taught to ignore these signals or push through them. Listening means you stop dismissing what your body knows and start taking it seriously.

Identify what is yours to carry and what is not. This is where you separate inherited patterns from chosen ones.

This is when you ask, *"Is this my anxiety or am I holding someone else's? Is this my responsibility or am I performing care to avoid conflict? Is this boundary mine to set or am I trying to control someone else's choices?"* Identification is not about judgment; it is about clarity. You cannot address what you have not named.

Soothe yourself structurally. Not with bubble baths or face masks — though those are fine but with the decisions that protect your nervous system.

Structural soothing looks like this in practice: a morning routine that gives your body ten minutes before it has to perform for anyone else, a boundary that means your phone stays out of the bedroom, a weekly check-in with yourself that asks not what I accomplished but how did I feel, a standing commitment to something that has nothing to do with output, whether that is a walk, a meal eaten slowly, or a conversation without an agenda. These are not luxuries. They are the infrastructure that keeps your nervous system from running on high alert all day. When you build a life that does not constantly dysregulate you, you spend less time recovering and more time living.

Sustain the practices when life gets hard because it will. Momentum will slip. The practices will be forgotten. Old patterns will return when everything piles up.

Sustaining means coming back even after you have stopped. And you will stop. Not because you are weak or because the work was not working, but because life does not pause to accommodate your growth. A hard season will arrive. The practices will fall away one by one, slowly and without announcement, until you look up and realize you have not checked in with yourself in weeks. That is not failure. That is what sustaining looks like, not seamless continuation but the willingness to return without making the absence mean something it does not. The practice did not disappear. You just set it down for a while. Pick it back up without interrogation.

These five movements are not linear. You do not master one and move to the next. They loop, layer, and inform each other. Some days you will breathe before you listen, identify before you soothe, and sustain by going back to breathing. The point is not perfection. It is practice. If you practice them long enough, something will change. The practices stop being something you must remember to do. They become the pulse you move to and the way you live.

That is the BLISS Rhythm, not a finish line or a reward for finally getting it right but a steady pulse that carries you once you get out of your own way. I see it now not in grand moments but in the ordinary ones, the ones that used to pass right through me without landing.

These are not the moments that make it onto Instagram. They are just ordinary moments in our lives. But that is exactly what the BLISS Rhythm is: choosing yourself in small ways until those small ways become the structure of your day, until rest is not something you earn and your boundaries are not rebellious acts but baseline expectations. The real work is learning to remain in moments that feel good without searching for the next fire to put out.

It is in the sunlight through the blinds. The laughter that interrupts a long day. The peace after forgiveness. The breath that says, "*I am okay right here.*"

The BLISS Rhythm is not something you achieve once and keep forever but something you tune into. Some days it will hum easily. Other days it will stutter. Hard weeks will still come. The practices will still be forgotten. What you built will still be tested when everything piles up.

And that is not failure. Bliss is not constant happiness or the absence of hard feelings. It is the capacity to stay present with whatever you feel without needing to escape it or override it. Regulation includes anger, grief, and frustration. The difference is you know how to move through them without abandoning yourself.

You know how to find your way back. Not because you are disciplined. Because your body remembers what it feels like to be okay.

And maybe that is what all of this has been leading to. The moment you stop chasing better and start experiencing here.

I think about the woman I was in Chapter One, standing in front of the mirror not recognizing myself, moving through days on autopilot, so disconnected I had forgotten what it felt like to just exist without performing. That woman is not gone. She is still a part of me, but she is not running the show anymore.

Your Turn

The BLISS Rhythm is not something you arrive at and stay. It is something you come back to, again and again, until coming back becomes second nature. These questions are asking what that looks like in your actual life right now, not the version you are planning toward, but the honest, present one. That is the only version worth examining.

1. Think about the last time you felt genuinely at ease. Not performing calm, not pretending to be fine, but relaxed. How long ago was it? What does that tell you?

2. Which of the five BLISS movements feels most foreign to you right now? Sit with that answer, it is telling you something.

3. Think about a moment this week when you could have paused but did not. What did your body do? What did you do instead?

4. If you built a life that did not require you to be depleted to be valuable, what would you have to give up? What identity would you have to let go of?

5. What does your BLISS Rhythm look like right now? Not the ideal version. The honest one. Where are you showing up for yourself and where are you still abandoning yourself to keep the peace?

Part Four
Living It

"Your story is what you have, what you will always have. It is something to own."

- Michelle Obama

Chapter 11
A Random Tuesday

I was driving down Ventura Boulevard on a Tuesday afternoon when *Cranes In The Sky* by Solange came on. The song I used to skip, the one that would pull me back to a version of myself I was still trying to understand. In the past I had to change the song or push through until it passed, every part of me already braced before the first verse ended.

But that day, with the windows cracked and the sun coming through the windshield at that angle where the whole city looks like it is glowing from the inside, the song played and something happened I almost did not notice.

The memory was there. My body knew it before my mind did. It started the way it always used to start. The brace. The tightening. The slow preparation for impact. I had learned to recognize this sequence and what always came next.

But this time nothing came.

My hand relaxed and I finished the exhale I had started. Something in me settled back without me telling it to. It just did.

And I realized something had changed. It was not from working harder or recovering faster or finally getting it right. It was from keeping the promise to return to myself, again and again, until my body started believing I would not leave it anymore.

I kept driving. The breeze coming through the window was perfect, that California sweetness where the air feels alive and generous, and you are thinking about nothing except that exact moment. The light hitting the palm trees. The city sounded the way it does on a Tuesday afternoon when traffic is light. Everything loosened when you are not running toward or away from something, just moving through your life.

There it was. A hum, a steady pulse that said, *"You are here. This is your life and you are finally living it."*

The mental checklist that usually ran in the background had gone still. The voice telling me what I should be doing was silent. The urgency pulling me toward the next task was gone. It was just the song playing and the warmth of the sun on my left arm and the realization I had been humming along without even noticing, genuinely happy on a random Tuesday, driving home from work with nothing special happening except the fact I was finally here for it.

Your moment will not look like mine. It will not be a Tuesday on Ventura Boulevard or a song by Solange. It will be something that belongs specifically to you, a commute, a meal, a drive home, a morning that does not demand anything yet. You will recognize it not because it is loud but because for the first time in a long time, you will not be waiting for it to end.

The smallest moments land differently when your body finally stops bracing for what used to hurt, a song on the radio, sun spilling through a window, stillness that finally feels like rest instead of a threat.

That week my friend called. She was going through something with a project at work, doubting herself, questioning the right call, second-guessing decisions she had already made. It was the kind of spiral I knew well and used to join her in without thinking.

Normally this would have been my job to fix. Dropping everything to stay on the phone for hours, absorbing every detail like it was my responsibility to solve, carrying it long after we hung up. Checking in three times that night because that is what showing up means, right? Good friends take on the weight and carry what you cannot.

But showing up does not mean disappearing and holding space does not mean holding everything.

Showing up looked like staying present without solving, asking her what she thought instead of telling her what to do, caring about her outcome without making it mine to fix.

She talked through what was happening and I listened, really listened. Not planning what I would say next, not searching for the perfect advice, not trying to fix it, minimize it, or rush her through the feeling. I just held space, letting her voice land without needing to fill every pause with a solution.

When she asked what I thought, I asked her back, "What do you think?"

There was a pause long enough that I wondered if she had wanted me to tell her what to do. But then she started figuring it out, talking through her options, naming what felt right and what felt forced, finding her own way through the mess. By the end of the call, she had worked it out. I had trusted her enough to find her own answers.

Before we hung up, she thanked me, said she felt clearer and knew what to do now.

The rest of the day moved normally. Lunch, emails, the unremarkable pace of the afternoon. I thought about her later with care, without that low-grade anxiety that says you are responsible for fixing everyone's problems, the kind of care that trusts people to handle their own lives.

I checked in the next morning to see how it went because I cared and wanted to know.

That is the difference. Showing up without taking on weight that is not mine to carry, holding space without disappearing into it, caring without losing myself in everyone else's struggles. Friendships actually feel better this way, lighter, more honest, and more sustainable when both people carry the weight of their own lives.

That same week I said no to drinks after work. Three coworkers were going and had been planning it all week. When they asked if I was coming, I felt the old pull, the one that says you should go even when you do not want to, that saying no makes you difficult, that people will stop inviting you if you are not always available.

I said, "Not tonight. But thanks for asking."

There was a pause that lasted maybe three seconds, but I felt it: the slight change in energy, the way one of them said "*okay*" in a way that meant something else, the way they kept talking, but the invitation did not come back around.

The familiar discomfort rose up immediately, the urge to explain and justify, to soften my *no* with an excuse that made it not about choosing rest but about some legitimate conflict I could not control. I wanted to say I was tired, that I had things to do, that maybe next time, anything to make it easier for them to not feel rejected.

But I did not.

I let the moment sit there, uncomfortable and unresolved. I went home, made dinner, sat on my couch. And that discomfort stayed with me for a while, the steady weight of having chosen myself at a small social cost, of knowing that boundary might mean fewer invitations, that protecting my energy might look like not being a team player.

I did not try to fix it, text the group later, or show up extra early the next day to prove I was still engaged. I just let it be what it was: a choice made, a boundary held, a small cost I was willing to pay.

That Friday I went to Chris' soccer game and sat on the metal bleachers with the other parents, the afternoon sun landing warm on the field, watching everything come alive. The grass had just been cut and the smell was everywhere, that specific green smell that meant someone had been taking care of something. Flowers bloomed along the edge of the field; bright yellow ones I did not know the name of but noticed anyway.

The kids were screaming. Running. Laughing in that full-body way kids do when they are thinking about nothing except the game in front of them. I just sat there, watching. Present. Chris ran down the field with his teammates. I noticed how fast he had gotten. How confident he was out there. How his whole face changed when he made a good pass. I was not thinking about what came next or what I should be doing instead. I just watched him play.

I thought about all the games I had sat through before, physically present but mentally absent, responding to emails, thinking about work, planning what came next. I had been there, but I had not been there.

But that day, I was all there. When he looked up at me from the field and waved, I waved back.

After the game we stopped for ice cream and sat outside at one of those little metal tables. He talked about the game, the goal he almost scored, his friend who got hurt but was okay. I listened, really listened, watching his face while he talked and noticing how animated he got when he explained what happened.

We did not rush or check the time. We just sat there eating ice cream and talking until we were done.

On the drive home, he fell asleep in the backseat. I looked at him through the rearview mirror, eight years old and growing up fast, and felt grateful I had not missed it.

After he was in bed, I sat on my couch with tea. The TV was off. My phone was in the other room. I just sat there with the stillness of a day I had actually been present for.

I realized something.

I was not tired.

I knew tired. The exhaustion that makes you feel like you are drowning even when you are sitting still, when your body feels heavy even when you are not doing anything, when your eyes burn even though you slept and irritability sits just under the surface waiting for someone to give you a reason to snap. The thought of one more conversation, one more decision, or one more anything making you want to disappear.

That tired used to live in me. I would sit on this same couch and feel like the day was still happening inside even though it was over, my mind unable to land, always processing, always waiting for the next thing to need me.

What I had spent years searching for had finally arrived, and there it was, on the couch, after a full day I had been present for.

That couch moment is not mine alone. It is available to you too, not at the end of a perfect week or after you get everything right, but after a day you chose to show up for. It will come without announcement. You will just feel it, the way I did, that what you have been carrying has gotten lighter. That you are still here. And that, right now, is its own kind of peace.

The days are still full, and life has not suddenly become easy, but the relationship with all of it has changed.

The adrenaline that used to keep me moving is gone. The performance of strength while falling apart inside is gone. And the measuring of my worth by how much I can carry without breaking is gone.

Hard days still come. Mornings when anxiety wakes me up before my alarm. Afternoons when I forget everything I have learned and fall back into old patterns. Weeks when holding it together feels like the best I can do.

I know how to come back now with honesty instead of shame or punishment. I can feel when I am abandoning myself now, and I can stop it. It does not happen perfectly or every time, but it happens often enough that everything has changed.

One morning I woke up early. The apartment was still, sun coming through the windows in that soft morning way. I made coffee and stood in my kitchen drinking it, looking out at the jacaranda tree, purple flowers covering the ground like a carpet.

I had walked past that window a hundred times without stopping.

That morning, I stopped.

That is what all of this has been building toward. A woman who knows how to come back, who can stand in her own kitchen on a regular morning and feel the full, unhurried beauty of a life she is living.

There is nowhere else I need to be.

Maybe you have already had a moment like this, or maybe it is still on its way. Either way it will not make a sound when it comes. It will just be there, the way all the important things are.

Your Turn

This is where you take stock. Not of how far you still have to go, but of how far you have already come. These questions are asking you to name what has changed in how you move through your days, how you treat yourself, and what you are no longer willing to accept. Do not minimize what is real. What you have built counts, even when it is ordinary.

1. Walk me through your version of a random Tuesday. Where does the BLISS Rhythm already show up without you thinking about it? Where is it still a conscious effort? Be specific about the day.

2. Where in your life are you showing up differently than you were a year ago? Name it specifically and without minimizing it.

3. Think about the last time you said no to something and did not apologize for it. How did it feel afterward? What did you do with the discomfort?

4. Is there someone you used to rescue who you now trust to figure things out on their own? What changed in you that made that possible?

5. What ordinary moment in your life, one that would never make it onto Instagram, has started to feel like enough?

Chapter 12
What Comes Next

You stayed.

The difference is not in forgetting, it is in the coming back. There will be a day when you realize you have been moving through your life on default for three days without noticing. You are inside demands instead of decisions, and you cannot remember when that happened. But then you feel it. That quality of being outside yourself. And instead of guilt, what arrives is something familiar. You have been here before, and you know exactly what to do with it. The work does not build immunity from drifting. It builds the ability to find your way back without making the drift mean something catastrophic about who you are.

Before you close this book and walk back into your life, I want to say something to you. What you have done here is not small. You kept going through the pages that made you want to look away. You sat with the questions that had no clean resolution. You did not stop when this work asked you to face things you had been moving past for years. That does not happen by accident. It happens because someone decided to stop running from themselves and kept making that decision even when it was hard. That someone is you.

The work is never easy. But it is not a battle either. It moves in waves, some of them long and steep, asking everything from you before they level out. You will move forward without being able to see what is waiting when the path opens. There will be stretches where the gains are invisible and the effort feels like it is going nowhere you can measure. In those stretches, trust this: the week you kept your appointment even though nothing felt like it was working, the morning you chose the walk instead of the scroll, the conversation where you held your ground even though giving in would have been simpler. Those are not small things. They are the whole thing.

Growth is not cinematic. It is repetitive and unglamorous, and it asks you to keep turning up even when nothing feels like it is happening. It is holding a limit for the fourth time with the same person, sitting in a session where nothing visible occurs but something reorganizes itself anyway, and reading a journal entry six months later and realizing how much you have grown. The small daily choices that do not feel significant while you are making them accumulate over time into a life that feels like yours.

There will be stretches where everything looks the same and you are doing all the right things and the return has not arrived yet. That flatness is not stagnation. It is what integration feels like from the inside. Maintenance does not look like momentum. It looks like turning up anyway.

Living this way costs something real. The relationships built on your depletion will register the change before you even name it. People who relied on your automatic yes and counted on your constant availability will experience your limits as proof that you are not the same. And some of them will be right because you are not. The person who said yes to everything and took on everyone's unease to keep the peace is becoming someone who knows the difference between love and labor and has learned that real generosity only exists when it is freely given rather than extracted. That is not a small thing. It is a different way of being alive.

The aftermath of holding that line is its own kind of work. Doubt will come with it. You will wonder if it was worth it and whether the version of you that would have just said yes would have been simpler for everyone. There is a loneliness in growth that nobody warns you about. Dynamics that used to feel like home will start to feel confining and rooms full of people will reveal themselves as spaces where you are no longer willing to shrink to fit. And choosing yourself when folding would have been so much easier will become the most clarifying thing you have ever done. Sit with that loneliness. It is not proof that you made the wrong choice. It is proof that you are finally making choices that are yours.

Grieving who you had to be to survive is part of this work. That person found a way to get through when getting through was the only option. Someone who responded to every request before their own, gave everything they had and then found more to give, and measured their value by how little they asked for and how much they delivered. Not weak. Doing everything, they knew how to do with what they had. You can hold gratitude for how far that person brought you while becoming someone who no longer must move through life that way. That is not betrayal. It is the most truthful thing you have ever done for yourself.

The people around you will respond to who you are becoming in ways you cannot fully predict. Some will find that when you stop shrinking yourself the connection grows into something neither of you could have accessed before because you were both too busy navigating the person you used to be. Others will drift toward someone who still operates the way you used to. That loss is real and it deserves to be felt. If you stay with it long enough, you will find what sits underneath: the quiet of a person who finally stopped making themselves smaller for spaces that were never built for their full size.

You will feel it before you can explain it. Walking into a room and sensing without hesitation where you stand. Saying no and not spending the next three hours replaying it. Sitting across from someone who used to make you smaller and finding they no longer have that access. That is not confidence in the way the world sells it. That is self-trust. It is quieter and more permanent, and it belongs entirely to you.

Self-trust compounds over time the way interest compounds in an account you stop monitoring because you know it is there. It showed up one evening when plans changed and I did not immediately spiral. I adjusted what needed adjusting, moved through the rest of the night, and let the other things wait until morning without punishing myself for it. That used to be impossible for me. Walking into rooms that once would have cost you everything will feel grounded rather than effortful, career decisions will come from what you truly want rather than what you fear will happen if you say no, and love will feel like a genuine choice instead of a carefully managed obligation. When you look at your life you will see it as yours, built by your hands, shaped by your values, belonging to no one else.

What surprised me most about living this way was not the ease. It was how I started seeing more clearly. Once you stop numbing yourself inside your own life a sharper kind of perception becomes available. You start distinguishing what really fills you from what has been draining you for years, feeling the difference between a yes that comes from desire and a yes that comes from obligation. You will be able to walk into any gathering and detect almost instantly whether there is an opening for you to be yourself or whether you will need to make yourself smaller to fit.

Nobody warns you that perceiving clearly can feel isolating at first. When you start seeing you cannot unsee. You spot the conversation that is about power dressed up as concern, the dynamic that only functions because you are doing all the absorbing, the friendship that has been running on your emotional investment for years without either of you acknowledging it. This does not make you superior. It makes you responsible for what you do with what you now know, for where you direct your focus, and for who you allow into your inner circle. That responsibility is not a burden. It is the first tangible evidence that you are someone who acts on what they see. That perception does not arrive with instructions. It develops through tuning into what your body has been trying to tell you and deciding that what it knows matters.

What you are cultivating inside yourself does not stay contained. It moves into how you love people, into how those closest to you feel being around you when you are fully grounded, into every connection that has room to deepen now that you have stopped shrinking inside it. The person doing this work is not only reshaping their own days. They are changing what becomes accessible in every room they enter and every person they encounter.

Hold onto how this period felt and who you were as you moved through it, the way your body understood the difference before your mind caught up. That knowing belongs to you. The more you allow yourself to inhabit that place, it will become your foundation rather than something you must keep chasing. One year from now you will be somewhere unremarkable, and you will see that the burden you used to haul everywhere is gone. It will not announce itself or arrive with any kind of ceremony. You will simply find that you are here, inside your own life, without needing to flee it. And you will know without anyone telling you that this is what all of it was for.

Be proud of yourself in the private way that requires no audience and no validation. Who you are growing into is real and deserves to be seen clearly by the one who has been there through all of it.

You.

Everything you need is already in you. It always was.

Epilogue

This is not an ending.

Life does not suddenly become simpler after this. The same responsibilities will be waiting when you close this book, and old habits may resurface. There will be days when you move too fast again, when you agree to things you do not actually want to do, when stillness feels strange or unfamiliar. That does not mean you missed the point. It means you are human and still living inside your own reality.

What changes is how you move through all of it.

She is still there in me sometimes, the woman who stood at the kitchen counter at midnight, holding everything together, believing the only way to be loved was to make herself impossible to leave. I understand why she did what she did. And I have learned to meet her with something I never offered her before.

I stopped giving from the bottom of myself. I stopped calling depletion loyalty and devotion. I stopped telling myself that giving until I had nothing left was the same thing as love. The feelings that used to take up permanent residence started moving through instead. They do not stay the way they used to.

Self-trust turned out to be steadier than I expected, not the confidence I imagined but something more grounded: the ability to let someone misread me without rushing to correct them, the willingness to be misunderstood instead of pretending to a certainty I do not owe anyone, the knowledge that my value was never tied to other people's approval.

The woman who kept the list, who said yes to everything, who carried the feelings of everyone around her to make sure no one was ever uneasy, she does not run my life anymore. When things get hard or when the old way feels safer than the honest one, she appears. She kept me alive through hard seasons that required her and she is not the enemy, but she no longer gets to make my decisions. I can love without losing myself in it now. I can rest without earning it first. I can be in a room without running it.

Some things stay hard, and that is true. Guilt still rises when you say no. Rest still feels wrong on days when output sounds like proof of worth. Hard no longer means broken. Resistance no longer means wrong. Tired no longer means insufficient. That is a small change, and it changes everything.

What matters now is the feeling you carry forward. The difference between being present and absent, between giving because you want to and giving because you are afraid, between your life and the pretending. That awareness lives in your body now. It waits for you, even when you forget it. You will always be able to find your way back to it.

There is no polished, figured-out person waiting on the other side of this. Just you, present in your own life even when it is hard, choosing yourself even when it costs something, resting before depletion instead of after.

Closing this book and returning to your life without urgency is allowed. Completion is not required. Proof is not necessary. The chase can stop.

Grace.

That is what all of this came down to. Not a framework or a practice or a set of rules. Just the slow work of learning to stop telling yourself you are fine when you are not. To let the life you are living be enough. To meet yourself there, exactly as you are.

That life is enough.

You are enough.

The way back stays clear. It always will.

Acknowledgments

This book would not exist without the people who believed in it before it was finished.

To my team, thank you for the time, talent, and care you poured into bringing this work to life. You showed up with excellence, and I am deeply grateful for each of you.

To my editor, thank you for your guidance, patience, and belief in this manuscript. Your insight sharpened these pages in ways I will always appreciate.

To Chris, you are the reason I do everything with intention. Watching you grow has taught me more about presence than any book ever could.

To my family and friends, thank you for carrying me through this process with your encouragement, love, and support, especially on the days when I struggled to carry myself.

And to every person who has ever held everything together while quietly coming apart inside, this book was written for you.

About the Author

Cherise Small, LCSW, is a therapist and founder of The Healing Point Therapy and Wellness in Los Angeles, California. Her work centers on emotional sustainability, self-trust, and helping people build lives they do not have to disappear inside to maintain.

Born and raised in Philadelphia, she brings together clinical insight, lived experience, and honest reflection to help people reconnect with themselves in a more grounded way. She earned her Master of Social Work from Widener University.

She has been featured on podcasts including Call Me CEO with Camille Walker, The Daring Well, and Black Girls Can Talk, and is a graduate of the Goldman Sachs One Million Black Women Black in Business program.

Cherise lives in Los Angeles with her son.

Website: release2heal.com

instagram.com/therapywithcherise

Reader Resources

Scan the code below to access your free reader resources, including the BLISS Framework Visual Toolkit and guided reflection sessions. For more, visit release2heal.com or find me on Instagram at @therapywithcherise.

The BLISS Rhythm

Breathe

Before you react. Before you say yes. Before you decide anything. Notice when your breath has gone shallow and let the exhale be longer than the inhale. That one adjustment signals your nervous system that it is safe to come down from high alert.

Listen

To what your body is telling you, not what you think it should be saying. Your body communicates in sensation. Tension. Restlessness. Flatness. A weight you cannot explain. These are not random. They are signals, and they have been there longer than you have been listening.

Identify

What is yours to carry and what is not. Ask whether what you are feeling belongs to you or if you picked it up somewhere else. Consider whether what you are managing is your responsibility or something you took on to keep the peace. Clarity here is not judgment. It is the beginning of relief.

Soothe

Not with temporary comfort, but with decisions that protect your nervous system over time. A boundary held. A morning that belongs to you before it belongs to anyone else. A standing commitment to something that has nothing to do with output or performance. These are not indulgences. They are how you stay well.

Sustain

The practice when life gets hard, because it will. Momentum will break. Old patterns will come back. You will go weeks without checking in with yourself and look up wondering how you got here again. That is not failure. Pick up where you left off without making the absence mean something it does not. The practice does not disappear when you set it down. It waits.

These five movements are not a sequence. They loop, layer, and return to each other.

Recommended Reading

The work in this book does not end here. If what you read opened something that needs more room than these pages can hold, the following are places to keep going.

If you are looking for a therapist

Psychology Today maintains a therapist directory searchable by location, specialty, and insurance. Visit:

psychologytoday.com/us/therapists.

Therapy for Black Girls (therapyforblackgirls.com) is a curated directory of Black therapists and mental health professionals, with community resources and a weekly podcast.

Open Path Collective (openpathcollective.org) connects people with therapists who offer reduced-fee sessions for those without insurance or with financial constraints.

If you are in crisis or need immediate support, call or text 988 to reach the Suicide and Crisis Lifeline, available around the clock, seven days a week.

Books worth reading alongside this one

Set Boundaries, Find Peace by Nedra Glover Tawwab. A New York Times bestseller and one of the most practical guides written on identifying, setting, and holding boundaries in every area of life. If Chapter 8 opened something for you, start here.

Drama Free by Nedra Glover Tawwab. A direct follow-up on navigating unhealthy family dynamics, including patterns of emotional unavailability and the relationships that ask the most of you. Connects directly to Chapter 4.

Rest Is Resistance by Tricia Hersey. A New York Times bestselling manifesto from the founder of The Nap Ministry on why rest is not a reward and how grind culture has specifically taken it from Black women. Essential reading after Chapter 5.

Sisterhood Heals by Dr. Joy Harden Bradford. From the licensed clinical psychologist and founder of the Therapy for Black Girls podcast, on how Black women build, repair, and sustain the friendships that keep them whole.

The Unapologetic Guide to Black Mental Health by Dr. Rheeda Walker. A practical guide to understanding mental wellness, navigating a system that was not built for you, and getting the care you deserve. For anyone ready to take their mental health seriously without apology.

www.ingramcontent.com/pod-product-compliance
Lightning Source LLC
LaVergne TN
LVHW050935210926
848482LV00013B/621
* 9 7 9 8 2 3 4 0 9 8 7 1 9 *